Praise for *Mind Over Marriage*

"Anyone who has summoned enough courage to enter into marriage knows how hard it can be. The plethora of self-help books on the subject indicates how desperately we need assistance if our marriages are going to thrive. In *Mind Over Marriage*, P. Gregg Blanton delivers a stunningly fresh perspective that not only is true to neuroscience, but equally faithful to the ancient Christian tradition of Centering Prayer. Weaving these two threads together, our guide delivers a beautiful tapestry of well-told stories, helpful translation of the latest research on the brain and relationships, and practical instruction. For those who long for deeper relationships with God and their spouse, I highly commend this work."

—Curt Thompson, MD, author of *Anatomy of the Soul*

"With clarity, logic, wisdom, and kindness, P. Gregg Blanton wraps his arms around you and your loved one and brings you together in a divine embrace. Step by step, he builds a foundation of understanding to help you enter into relationships with more safety, trust, and confidence. In each chapter of this easy-to-digest book, he shows you the way toward more wholesome intimacy in your life. The powerful skills this book teaches will help me and my wife in our marriage. I believe it will do the same for you."

—Joshua Ehrlich, PhD, chairman of the
Global Leadership Council and author of *Mindshifting*

"Dr. P. Gregg Blanton brings together science and spirituality in a way that is sure to be helpful to many clients. He explains brain science in a way that is easy to understand, and he helps us understand contemplative prayer as a means to closeness for couples. Exercises in the book allow couples to engage in practices between sessions that promote connection and intimacy. Overall, I think this book will impact the profession, adding a scientific explanation of the importance of our spiritual life."　　　　　　　　—Jon Winek, PhD, director of the Marriage and Family Therapy Program at Appalachian State University and author of *Systemic Family Therapy*

"In *Mind Over Marriage,* a veteran marriage and family therapist suggests that the primary cause for relationship problems may be found within the minds of those who are in conflict. The suggested solution for this assertion points the field in a new direction. This is a well-written and important book."

—Gary W. Moon, MDiv, PhD, executive director of the Dallas Willard Center for Christian Spiritual Formation and author of *Apprenticeship with Jesus*

"Seldom do good science and good spirituality come together so well—and to support good relationships besides! We are learning that emotional sobriety does not come about without the help of some form of the contemplative mind. Well, here is a good teacher of all of the above."　　　　　　　　—Father Richard Rohr, OFM, founder of the Center for Action and Contemplation and author of *Immortal Diamond*

"In *Mind Over Marriage,* P. Gregg Blanton suggests that transformation in marriage is enhanced through a regular practice of centering prayer. Blanton points out that scientific studies have indicated that a commitment to a contemplative practice opens individuals to new ways of communicating. This thoughtful book will open your eyes, ears, and heart to a new way of being in marriage which is centered in God."　　　　　　　　—Gail Fitzpatrick-Hopler, president of Contemplative Outreach, Ltd.

MIND OVER MARRIAGE

TRANSFORMING YOUR RELATIONSHIP
USING CENTERING PRAYER AND NEUROSCIENCE

P. GREGG BLANTON

Lantern Books | *New York*

A DIVISION OF BOOKLIGHT, INC.

2013
Lantern Books
128 Second Place
Brooklyn, NY 11231
www.lanternbooks.com

Printed in the United States of America

Library of Congress Cataloging-in-Publication Data

Blanton, P. Gregg.
Mind over marriage : transforming your relationship
using centering prayer and neuroscience / P. Gregg Blanton.
pages cm
ISBN 978-1-59056-375-5 (pbk. : alk. paper) — ISBN 978-1-59056-376-2 (ebook)
1. Marriage—Religious aspects—Christianity. 2. Contemplation.
3. Prayer—Christianity. 4. Neurosciences—Religious aspects—Christianity.
I. Title.
BV835.B57 2013
248.8'44—dc23
2012046020

Contents

Introduction

The couple sitting across from me was playing the oldest game in human history: the blame game. Like so many couples I have seen before, Steve and Linda were defining their relationship problem in terms of the other person. Steve, a creative architect, saw their difficulty as resulting from Linda's "selfishness and self-centeredness," while Linda, a successful lawyer, viewed Steve's "bullying" behavior as the source of their marital unhappiness.

At that moment, in my imagination, I could see each one of them being overwhelmed by a flood of emotions. And this wave of feelings was pushing them into memories, thoughts, and actions that were detrimental to their marital relationship. I was convinced that they would have chosen other behaviors, ones that would have protected their marriage, if they had been in their "right minds."

It saddened but did not surprise me to witness Steve and Linda stepping into a familiar mental trap; that is, defining the marital problem in terms of the other person. This response seems to be an ancient means of self-defense. According to Christian thought, the first committed couple engaged in this form of behavior. In Genesis, we read that when Adam and Eve got into trouble, Adam was quick to point an accusing finger at his wife (Genesis 3:12). And just like Adam, Eve readily created a narrative that cast herself in the role of victim, putting someone else in the role of villain (Genesis 3:13).

I have heard it said that how you start determines how you finish. Well, Steve and Linda were picking the wrong place—the other person—to start working on the cause and solution of their marital woes. Andrew Christensen and Neil Jacobson, both professors of psychology and co-creators of a counseling model called Integrative Behavioral Couple Therapy (IBCT), phrase it in a slightly different manner, saying that the way we understand a problem determines the way we cope with it.[1] Now, if we define the relationship difficulty as resulting from something our spouse does, then we will naturally demand a change in our partner. However, we have all discovered that accusing the one we love of wrong actions and character flaws rarely elicits the change we desire.

If we resist the urge to lay the blame on our spouse, then where do we start? How do we begin to understand the unhappiness that may exist in our marriage? Both modern scientific findings and the ancient Christian contemplative tradition point us in the same direction for answers to these questions. They suggest that, instead of looking outside for a culprit, we look inside. Perhaps the root of our marital problems lies as close as our own mind.

As Christensen and Jacobson suggest, identifying our own mind as the basic cause of marital problems points us in a new direction for change. Identifying and exploring this new direction is the purpose of this book. First, we will attempt to understand how the ordinary mind works and how these mental functions affect our marital relationship. Then we will set out to describe how to retrain the mind through a specific contemplative practice called Centering Prayer. Centering Prayer is a contemporary version of the ancient Christian custom of contemplation. In the process of exploring Centering Prayer, we will identify new skills and abilities that grow out of a regular contemplative practice. Finally, we will develop a plan for improving our marriage through the application of these new skills and the development of new behavioral traits.

In this book, we will examine the topics of mind and marriage through the lens of both Christian contemplative thought and scientific discoveries. Turning to science, we will look more specifically at recent findings from psychology, the science of human behavior, and neuroscience, the science of the brain. Turning to Christian contemplative thought, we will explore ideas that go back 2,000 years. Even though Christian contemplative thought precedes scientific thought, we will see the two streams of knowledge converge at the points of minds and marriages. By emphasizing an approach of mind over marriage, we will develop useful strategies that allow us to change our minds so that we can change our marriages.

This book is built upon three positive assumptions about a dialogue between Christian contemplative and scientific thought: First, the discoveries these two disciplines have made about minds and marriages are often similar and almost always complement each other. Second, because scientific and contemplative findings are complementary approaches to our study of minds and marriages, we do not have to choose one field over the other. Finally, a conversation between these two approaches to knowledge should yield valuable insights into the cause of marital unhappiness—the mind.

If we adopt the position that our mind is the cause of marital unhappiness—and I believe that it is—then we must start with some understanding of the mind itself. Let's start with some definitions of the mind. Gerald May, a Christian psychiatrist and contemplative, suggests that the mind is not a thing, nor is it a place in any physical sense.[2] Rather, the mind consists of a variety of activities or processes that are performed by the brain in conjunction with other parts of the nervous system and the body. In the field of neuroscience, Daniel Siegel, a professor of psychiatry at the UCLA School of Medicine, also draws a connection between the brain and the mind.[3] According to Siegel, the brain—the extended nervous system that is distributed throughout the entire body—produces a flow of energy and information. The mind, then, in part, is what regulates this flow of energy and information. These definitions, one from a Christian contemplative and the other from an expert in neuroscience, point to the interaction between the brain and the mind. If we bring our marriage into the equation, then

Siegel suggests that how we share the flow of energy and information with our spouse directly affects our marital relationship and happiness.

Let's return to Steve and Linda and see what was actually happening as they sat there in my office. Even though I couldn't read their minds, I had some pretty good ideas about what was going on. I believe that Steve and Linda's minds were first tipped out of balance by a sense of disconnection and insecurity. I assume each of them had done something that was perceived by their partner as being hurtful or uncaring. We know now that if something happens to undermine our need for security, our mind begins to fall under the control of forgotten memories, uncontrollable emotions, and destructive actions.

Whenever we feel distant from our spouse, a warning signal of insecurity is sounded, and then an entire cascade of mental processes follows. Perhaps this announcement of danger was at the root of Steve and Linda's behavior. According to Paul Gilbert, a British psychologist, this alarm is activated by the mind's threat and self-protective system.[4] This threat system has been designed along fairly simple lines: to detect danger and to protect us. When a risk to our security is noticed, the emotion of fear quickly surfaces. And then, this state of fear begins to direct our narratives and behavior, and numerous problems can happen.

According to Daniel Siegel, when the mind gets out of balance, it moves toward either chaos (over-arousal) or rigidity (under-arousal).[5] Looking at the faces of Steve and Linda, I was sure that both of their minds were in a state of chaos. As a result, they were lost in intense memories, disruptive emotions, irrational thoughts, and impulsive behaviors. As John O'Donohue, an Irish poet and Christian contemplative, would say, they had become trapped in a mental prison. The mind of each had become a "small room without a light."[6] We will explore how we get caught up—or trapped—in these mental processes in the first part of this book.

Scientists and Christian contemplatives put it in different ways, but both disciplines recognize the need to restore balance to our minds.

In order to bring this balance, scientists such as Daniel Siegel and Paul Gilbert advocate training the mind, replacing old mental functions with new ones, or freeing our mind from old mental patterns.[7] Similarly, Christian contemplatives talk about purifying, refining, emptying, opening, freeing, or liberating the mind.[8] Richard Rohr, a Christian contemplative, says that we can restore balance to our minds by changing our minds.[9] Rohr points out that Jesus' very first message in the Gospels, which is usually translated as "convert," "repent," or "reform," (Matthew 4:17; Mark 1:15) is the Greek word *metanoia*, which literally means to "change your mind."

The insights that Christian contemplative and scientific thinkers give us into the workings of the mind and how these mental processes impact our marital relationships give rise to important questions. How do we restore balance to our turbulent or sluggish minds? How do we calm the threat-based system of the mind that prompts us to attack our spouse, close off, or shut down? Instead of being pushed around by fear, how can we love our spouse the way we really want to? How can we make a mental shift from fear to one of love?

In the last three decades, science has begun to echo an old Christian answer to the question of how to change or liberate the mind. The answer is through contemplative practice. Daniel Siegel points toward a growing body of research that demonstrates that contemplative practices can strengthen minds and interpersonal relationships.[10]

According to Siegel, scientific studies support the idea that contemplative skills can move our mind toward greater health. And by creating balance in our mind, we can then form a better connection with our spouse. Research clearly shows that transforming our minds through contemplative skills creates well-being in our marital relationships.[11]

The contemplative practice that we find within the Christian tradition is called contemplative prayer. According to John O'Donohue, contemplative prayer is the key that liberates us from the mental prison in which we too often find ourselves.[12] In order to clear up some of the misunderstanding associated with contemplative prayer, David Benner, a Christian psychologist and contemplative, offers us some basic instruction.[13] In essence, he says, contemplative prayer is simply being with God in wordless communion. The goal of contemplative prayer is being open to God, turning to God in faith. The rest is up to God.

When I suggested to Steve and Linda that contemplative prayer could possibly not only change their minds, but change their marriage—and I was happy to say that my claims had scientific backing—they were immediately interested. They were eager to know how it worked, so I told them that I would teach them a simple method of contemplative prayer called Centering Prayer. Thomas Keating, the principal architect and spokesperson for Centering Prayer, says that Centering Prayer is an attempt to present contemplative prayer in an up-to-date form, one that puts a certain order and method to it.[14]

How can Steve and Linda hope to benefit from engaging in Centering Prayer on a consistent basis? What skills and qualities can they expect to develop as they enter into a regular contemplative practice? In the second part of this book, we will see how contemplative prayer teaches us to be still, attentive, open, and detached. With these skills, we can move toward the ultimate goals of contemplation: union and love.

Contemplative prayer, in which we spend time with God, has transformational possibilities. According to Richard Rohr, transformation is a type of journey, one that starts with knowing where we are and a willingness to go someplace else.[15] Contemplative prayer can take us from chaos to stillness, from distraction to attention, from rigidity to openness, from attachment to letting go, from the illusion of separateness to union, and from fear to love. This was a transformation that Steve and Linda desired. They wanted to embark on a journey that had the power to change their minds, and thus their marriage.

The last section of this book brings to light this idea: changing our mind can change our marriage. We will discover how the six skills that are examined in the second part of this book—stillness, attention, openness, letting go, union, and love—are six traits that can meaningfully impact the health and strength of our marriage. Each trait is associated with a specific skill. Stillness gives rise to the trait of calmness, attention produces attunement, openness leads to the quality of presence, letting go helps us learn how to reconstruct our narratives, union gives rise to resonance, and love enables us to trust. The development and application of these behavioral traits—calmness, attunement, presence, storytelling, resonance, and trust—provide us with the tools we need for rebuilding a secure and happy marriage.

Everything in this book rests on three fundamental principles. The first, addressed in part I, is that changing our mind begins with a thorough understanding of how the ordinary mind works. This first section will rely equally upon scientific and Christian contemplative findings. Part II illustrates the second principle that contemplative practice is a learnable skill that can alter the way the mind functions. Here, we will draw primarily upon Christian contemplative thought in general, and Centering Prayer in particular. The third principle, in part III, is at the heart of my work as a marriage counselor. Well-being occurs in a marriage as we develop the traits that emerge from a regular practice of contemplative prayer. This last section of the book depends largely upon scientific thought, but also appeals to Christian contemplative ideas.

Are you willing to work on your marriage by starting with your own mind? Do you want to learn how to bring healing to both your mind and your marriage through Christian contemplative prayer? Are you eager to learn how to move your mind from a place of fear to one of love? If so, this book will help guide you on your journey.

Let's begin by taking a survey of the chapters that lie ahead:

Chapter 1, Separation: In this chapter, we will see how the mind is wired for connection. When this longing for attachment is denied in our marriage, we manifest different patterns of insecurity. This feeling of insecurity activates the mind toward either chaos or rigidity. A sense of separation engages our mind's threat response system, which then activates memories, physiological sensations, emotions, narratives, and behavioral reactions. When these responses get out of hand, they can cause all kinds of problems for our marriage.

Chapter 2, Self: The workings of the mind would be completely in the dark without the self. The self, that thing we carry around inside that allows us to witness the flow of our mind, helps us experience our memories, emotions, and thoughts. In spite of its usefulness, the self also carries with it certain deficiencies that can threaten the health of our marriage. In this chapter, we will identify these limitations.

Chapter 3, Body: In this chapter, we will examine the connection between the body and the mind. Once the self-protection system of the mind picks up on a threat, it activates the body to take action against the perceived danger. When we experience our spouse as that risk to our safety, our body becomes keyed up, this reaction can get out of hand, and then we are at war with our spouse. Studies show that this physiological arousal can almost perfectly predict a decline in our marital satisfaction.16

Chapter 4, Memories: Memory comes in two different forms: totally conscious, or outside of our awareness. The memories that operate below our awareness, implicit memories, are at the very core of how we interact with our spouse. In this chapter, we will learn how implicit memories are activated and what happens once they are. In the presence of a perceived threat, memories can quickly arouse old fears, strong physical sensations, and automatic protective behaviors.

Chapter 5, Emotions: In this chapter, we will explore the threat-based emotion of fear. Starting with the neurobiology of fear, we will describe how fear is activated and then how it works with memories, narratives, and protective actions. Thomas Merton, the famous Christian contemplative, says: "At the root of all war is fear."[17] Sometimes, fear causes us to see our spouse as a threat and the enemy, and as a result, we feel overwhelmed with emotions. Being flooded with feelings can cause us to say and do things we later regret.

Chapter 6, Narratives: What story do you have about your spouse and your marriage? This narrative will probably determine the outcome of your marriage. Research shows us that unhappy couples develop stories that support their fear of their spouse. "Look at how my spouse feels, thinks, and acts! Of course I should be afraid!" In this chapter, we will study how our narratives are activated and constructed. We will see what happens when a narrative comes under the influence of fear.

Chapter 7, Behavior: In a state of threat, the mind prepares for war, not love. When we become upset and aroused, our mind pushes us to act in negative ways. In this chapter, we will examine our tendency to fight with our spouse, flee, or shut down. Studies show that unhappy couples, in a state of emotional and physical arousal, get caught up in patterns of behavior that are detrimental to the relationship. We will explore the most painful and common patterns of interacting.

Chapter 8, Contemplative Prayer: How do we restore the mind to balance? In the last three decades, science has begun to echo an old Christian answer to this question—that is, through contemplative prayer. What are the characteristics of the "inner room" that we enter through Centering Prayer? What does the normal mind do during this practice? What happens when the mind refrains from its normal activities? What are the mental skills that we develop through contemplative prayer? All of these questions are addressed in this chapter.

Chapter 9, Stillness: According to John O'Donohue, the tools of contemplative prayer are stillness and silence.[18] Father Thomas Keating says that Centering Prayer is patterned on the comparison given by Jesus that prayer is like going into your room and closing the door (Matthew 6:6).[19] This concept may sound simple, but learning to sit in a room, alone with your mind, for twenty minutes can be quite challenging. Richard Rohr says, "You will want to run, I assure you."[20] Alan Wallace, a philosopher, quotes writer Anne Lamott as saying, "My mind is like a bad neighborhood, I try not to go there alone."[21] We will want to run because of all the negative thoughts, painful memories, and turbulent emotions that emerge in this place of quiet. We will discover how restless the mind really is. However, in stillness, the flow of our mind begins to slow down. As we willingly shut off the chatter of our mind, we begin to notice the still, small voice of God (Psalms 46:10).

Chapter 10, Attention: When we are silent and still, we start developing the ability to pay attention in a special way. Usually, our attention is captured by the mental patterns of our mind: emotions, memories, and commentaries on events. And once these ordinary mental processes kidnap our attention, we find ourselves reacting in a grasping (maintaining the thought) or rejecting (pushing the thought away) manner. However, Centering Prayer is designed to help us withdraw our attention from the ordinary flow of mental patterns. We are not trying to stop or prevent thoughts, feelings, and memories. Instead, we are learning to notice the thought, sense it, welcome it, and then leave it alone. Attention is a state of active receptivity.

Chapter 11, Openness: Paying attention in this way leads us to the next skill: openness. Without mental training through contemplative practice, our first instinct is to change or control the activities of our mind. We may hold on to pleasant thoughts, feelings, and memories, while we push away the unpleasant ones. However, openness is the ability to accept whatever our mind brings us in the present moment. Nothing is shut out, eliminated, or excluded. Instead, we open our awareness to all our mental processes, so that we can notice them and then leave them alone. By leaving them alone, we can engage in the purpose of Centering Prayer, openness to God.

Chapter 12, Letting Go: As we repeatedly enter into the inner room of prayer, we are learning to let go. This idea implies that there are things we want to hold on to, but what are we most attached to? Our own urges, feelings, and commentaries. We are attached to our view of our spouse or our marriage. Our view must be right. But the principle discipline of Centering Prayer is learning to detach or let go. Letting go allows us to watch our mental processes without getting swept up in them, without letting our attention get kidnapped. This ability to let go is counterintuitive because we naturally want to hold on to things we value, but emptying ourselves of old mental processes allows us to be filled with new ones.

Chapter 13, Union: The goal of contemplative prayer is the realization of one's essential union with God. Keating describes contemplative prayer as "a process of interior transformation, a conversation initiated by God and leading, if we consent, to divine union."[22] The skills engendered through a regular contemplative practice prepare but don't entitle us to the gift of union. Hopefully, Centering Prayer allows us to reach a deeper level of the mind, a level where we become awake to another dimension of reality. At this level, we may sense on occasions that we really are not separate from God, as our ordinary minds would suggest. Instead, just as the air we breathe is in and around us, we are awakened to the presence of God that penetrates us and is all around us.

Chapter 14, Love: Ultimately, through contemplative practice, our mind gradually begins shifting from a position of fear to one of love. This one essential quality of contemplation—love—is affirmed by all Christian contemplatives. However, according to the Christian contemplative tradition, just like divine union, love cannot be achieved by human effort. Instead, the ability to love comes to us by God. As we open ourselves to God in Centering Prayer, as we empty our mind of old mental properties, we become open to being filled with love.

Chapter 15, The Science of Contemplation: For insights into how Centering Prayer can benefit our marriage, we must turn to science. Most recent scientific research is focused on a contemplative practice called mindfulness. Even though Centering Prayer has not garnered this same attention from the scientific community, research findings indicate that we can apply the discoveries about mindfulness to Centering Prayer. The new science of contemplation is now telling us that through a regular contemplative practice, we can cultivate certain personal traits that can transform our life and marriage.

Chapter 16, Calmness: Research is showing that there is a direct relationship between calmness and marital satisfaction.[23] The findings reveal that our marital happiness declines as our heart rate increases. How do we go about calming our own and our spouse's physiology? There is scientific evidence that supports a connection between contemplative practice and one's ability to calm one's mind—what many researchers refer to as emotional regulation. It seems that the ability to self-soothe and soothe one's partner are central to marital happiness. Secure couples rely upon interactive regulation.[24] In this chapter, we will not only learn ways to self-soothe, but also strategies for soothing our spouse.

Chapter 17, Attunement: Behavioral scientists, such as Daniel Siegel, Marion Solomon, professor in the Department of Psychiatry at UCLA, and Stan Tatkin, developer of the Psychological Approach to Couple Therapy, point to the connection between contemplative practice and attunement.[25] They say that attunement, how we focus our attention on our spouse, is necessary if we are going to feel safe and secure in our marital relationships. John Gottman, a leading psychologist known for his work with couples, offers us the acronym ATTUNE to help us understand the elements of attunement.[26]

Chapter 18, Presence: Scientific studies show that contemplative practice is particularly useful for promoting the trait of presence. Presence, defined as a state of being open, allows us to remain receptive to our partner. It is a way of being that we bring to our marriage.[27] It is an attitude or stance toward the present moment that allows us to attend openly and clearly to both our own experience and that of our spouse. Out of this openness, we can respond appropriately to the interaction that we are having with our spouse.

Chapter 19, Stories of Truth: According to John Gottman, the story-of-us—the one about our partner and our relationship—is an index of what will eventually happen to our marriage.[28] Obviously, our ability to tell positive stories is essential to the health of our relationship. Our goal in this chapter is to learn how to create good stories. These stories focus on vulnerabilities, center on understanding emotions, emphasize good times together, and maximize our partner's positive qualities. If

PART I

Understanding
Your
Mind

CHAPTER I

Separation

One is the loneliest, number one is the loneliest
Number one is the loneliest number that you'll ever do
One is the loneliest, one is the loneliest
One is the loneliest number that you'll ever do
It's just no good anymore since she went away
—*Three Dog Night*

There can be no union without separation.
—*John O'Donohue, Eternal Echoes*

Let's begin our journey into minds and marriages by examining two critical concepts: separation and union. According to both scientific and Christian contemplative thought, our experiences of disconnecting from and then reconnecting with loved ones determine the stability of both our mind and our most intimate relationships. Thinkers from both disciplines observe that we are wired for connection but that this innate need is often thwarted. Instead of feeling wanted, cherished, and nurtured, we wind up feeling alone and lonely. This experience of being separate, lonesome, and disconnected not only undermines the development of our mind, but also the health of our marriage.

A problem with separating and reuniting lies at the root of most unhappy marriages, according to Marion Solomon and Stan Tatkin, both marriage counselors.[32] This difficulty was evident in the story told to me by my patients Brad and Katie. They both complained about the uncomfortable experience of coming home and feeling disconnected after a hard day at work. Katie, a thirty-eight-year-old nurse, said that her two children met her at the door, but that Brad was nowhere to be found. They both agreed that he was usually downstairs about that time, playing games on his computer. "Why doesn't he greet me at the door with a hug and kiss the way he used to?" she asked. They used to provide each other with a warm welcome, but this habit had disappeared during the past ten months. According to Brad, a medical equipment salesman, Katie usually came home irritated about something at work and "she would take it out on me." He wished he could do something to make her feel better, but he felt unable to give her the "right answer." As a result, he found it easier to just let her come home and start her evening routine. They both agreed that they were beginning to feel more like roommates than marriage partners.

Like all couples who feel separate and lonely, Brad and Katie each desperately longed to feel like they fit in, like they were part of a team. They wanted to belong. For centuries, Christian contemplatives have recognized this deep desire for belonging. No one wants to be isolated or excluded, but a sense of alienation seems endemic to the human condition. According to Father Thomas Keating, the concept of original sin addresses this feeling of being cut off from God, other people, and the true self.[33] Christian contemplatives point to the story in Genesis of Adam and Eve's expulsion from the garden as a terrifying image of what it is like to be excluded from belonging. On the other hand, the most beautiful image in the Bible is of heaven: a place of total belonging, a place where there is no separation.[34]

Consistent with Christian contemplative thought, this sense of separation that we feel with God and even our marriage partner is a grand illusion generated by the mind.[35] The mind insists on seeing a wall of separation between self and God, self and marriage partner. The mind tells us that we are over here and that God—or our spouse—is over there. The gap between us seems to be a great distance that we cannot bridge.

Christian contemplatives maintain that the outcome of this sense of separation is insecurity. Father Thomas Keating says that a relationship with God could or should make us feel secure; however, for many of us, this experience of union with God is missing.[36] As a result, instead of feeling secure, we feel vulnerable and threatened. Instead of feeling loved, we experience intense fear. We may turn to our marriage partner for a sense of connection, but our anxiety about being alone is reignited when we feel emotionally distant from our spouse. Experiences of being criticized, excluded, and unwanted arouse our deepest fears.

I heard this fear in Katie's voice as she described her relationship with Brad. Katie expressed her dismay upon finding out that Brad had been masturbating on a regular basis while she was away at work. For the past three weeks, Brad had not initiated any physical intimacy with her, even though she had told him of her desire for sex. Katie felt confused, lonely, and unwanted. Exasperated, she asked, "Isn't this something we're supposed to do together?"

Katie's desire for security and connection is recognized within the Christian contemplative tradition as well as the discipline of psychology. One of the early pioneers to identify and write about the power of separation and union to shape our minds and intimate relationships was a psychiatrist named John Bowlby. His approach, called attachment theory, emerged out of his work with children who were made homeless in the aftermath of World War II and with toddlers who were separated from their parents by prolonged hospitalization or institutionalization. Bowlby helped us recognize that from the day we are born, our minds are designed to respond to the care and kindness of others.

Mary Ainsworth, a psychologist, joined Bowlby with his research in the 1950s, and her experiments with separations and reunions between mothers and infants greatly increased our knowledge of attachment.[37] By putting infants in a "strange situation," Ainsworth was able to identify several distinct types of attachments between mothers and their children. In her investigations, she exposed infants to two separations, two reunions, and exposure to a stranger (a trained baby watcher). Based upon her observations of how infants responded to these disconnections and reconnections with their mothers, Ainsworth identified two major types of attachment: secure and insecure. Secure infants, who were distressed during the separation, expressed a need for comfort after separation and were relieved by the soothing they received upon reunion. The insecure pattern of attachment, which Ainsworth subdivided into anxious and avoidant types, displayed a different set of responses upon separation and reunion. Avoidant infants appeared calm on the outside during the separation (even though tests showed that they were physiologically aroused on the inside) and they did not invite any connection with their mothers upon seeing them again. On the other hand, the anxious children remained extremely upset during the separation and experienced limited relief upon reunion.

You may be thinking, "What does this research about infants and their mothers have to do with me and my marriage?" Well, scientific research confirms a high correlation between early attachment categories and adult attachment patterns. In other words, how you dealt with disconnections and reconnections as a child is most likely how you will respond to them today in your marriage. When you were growing up, were your parents able to soothe and reassure you when you were upset? Were you eager for their comfort or did you avoid your parents when you were disturbed? Did you calm down and feel better upon being reunited with your parents after a frightening experience? The patterns you established regarding separations and reunions as a child have probably followed you into your marriage.

Katie's childhood patterns had accompanied her into her marriage. As a young girl her parents divorced, and soon thereafter she found herself in the custody of her dad and her new stepmother. Her step-mother—whom she found to be cold and uncaring—stayed at home to take care of Katie and her little sister while her dad went off to work.

She waited eagerly for her dad's return after work, and she relished the times she spent with her biological mother on the weekends. She frequently wanted reassurance and asked her parents, "Do you love me?" Their words of love and their hugs felt good, but their actions never seemed to put her mind totally at rest.

Now that she was married, Katie experienced this same set of interactions. Reuniting with her husband in the evenings was important to Katie. Bedtime was particularly significant to her, and lying close to Brad was especially comforting and calming. This is where they had a problem, though. Katie complained that Brad sometimes went to bed later than she did. On these occasions, it was difficult for her to drift off to sleep. Something was missing. In addition, when Brad got in bed, if she moved over to touch him, he typically moved away and turned his back. This sense of separation at the end of the day was hard to bear. Katie wanted to feel connected.

A sense of connection, according to both Christian contemplative and scientific thinkers, keeps our mind in balance. However, when we feel mistreated or misunderstood by our spouse, our mind can quickly move out of balance. Feeling excluded and separate can push our mind toward either chaos or rigidity. In chaos, we often feel angry and do things that hurt our spouse, whereas in rigidity, we typically just want to withdraw from and not communicate with our partner. Either way, we find ourselves in a state of mind that interferes with our ability to react to our spouse in a way that predicts relationship success.

I witnessed these two mental patterns—chaos and rigidity—in my office recently during a conversation with Lisa and Bill. Lisa, the owner of a small business, became agitated when Bill, a building contractor, complained about a broken promise. Lisa, who made her living off of talking, responded with a barrage of words. She was saying a lot, but her response was not related to Bill's concern. Glancing over at Bill, I could tell that he had simply given up on the conversation. When I asked them to reflect upon their internal experience and interpersonal behavior, Lisa surprised me by acknowledging that her words were self-protective. "Talking is my delay tactic while I try to figure out how to best defend myself," she admitted. Bill seemed relieved to hear her say that and he responded, "Yeah, I felt like you were using your words to build a wall between us." With their minds out of balance, they were finding it difficult to reconnect.

Being cut off from the one we love pushes the mind out of balance because separation is experienced as a dangerous situation. According to both scientific and Christian contemplative thought, anything that puts our sense of connection and security in jeopardy activates an important property of the mind: the threat response system. When our spouse responds to us with unkind words, disinterested looks, and insensitive behaviors, an alarm goes off in our threat system, telling us that our spouse is the enemy. When we feel pushed away, undesired, or unwanted by our spouse, our mind begins to organize for war, not love.[38]

Once the threat response system is activated, a predictable network of mental functions begins to fall in place. I observed this series of mental events as recently as the other day when my wife was unresponsive to my request for help on a house project. Within seconds, my body felt energized, I became angry, and I began to say things I regretted later. Both scientists and contemplatives would agree that two other important mental properties—memory and narrative—were joining in this cascade of physiological, emotional, and behavioral responses. My mind was clearly caught up and directed by this threat response system.

The threat response system is activated when we feel disconnected for too long from the spouse we love. Of course, being separated is inevitable in a marital relationship. Some of these times apart are chosen and accepted by both partners, such as going to work, going to sleep, or attending a professional meeting. At other times, we end up feeling isolated from our spouse because of a hurtful experience, such as a failure to respond with care and understanding to an important need. Or perhaps we wind up feeling unwanted, like Bill did when Lisa went to the beach with some girlfriends and stayed an extra day, not considering his input. When Lisa complained that Bill was trying to control her, he replied, "That's not it at all. I'm just afraid that we are losing a sense of us." Both Christian contemplative and scientific thinkers agree that the antidote for feelings of separation is reunion.

However, if reunion does not occur, the threat response system gets caught up in a program of self-protection or protection of the self. The self is essential to our understanding of the mind, because it is the process that allows us to witness our mental functions: emotions, memories, thinking, and behavior. The self identifies with these activities of the mind and says, "These are my feelings, my memories, and my thoughts, and this is what I should do!" Once the self is threatened, the mind sets out to protect it. In the next chapter, we will explore this important process—the self—that works in tandem with the mind.

Try this:

Stand on the opposite side of the room from your partner. Face each other and maintain eye contact at all times. Do not talk. You can laugh all you want, but do not talk. Try to keep your hands and arms at your sides most of the time.

Designate yourself to be the "walker" while your partner stands still. Start walking slowly toward your partner and stop at a desired point. Where and why you stop is up to you. You can base it on how you feel or what you see on your spouse's face. After you come to a stop, your partner may motion for you to move forward or backward until he or she feels the distance is right.

Now leave the room for a few seconds. Once you re-enter the room, move toward your spouse—but this time do something that seems invasive. In other words, get so close it makes your spouse uncomfortable. Sustain this position for a moment. Your spouse can now correct (with motions, not words) the distance so that he or she feels completely relaxed. Now, embrace each other for a moment as if you are reuniting after a long separation.

　　Last, change positions and repeat the exercise. Your partner will now be walking while you stand in place.[39]

Questions to ponder:

1. How did you make your decision to stop walking toward your spouse? (Was it something you felt? Did your spouse do something?)

2. When you were in the stationary role, how did you respond when your spouse was approaching?

3. Who wanted more distance? More closeness? If you wanted more closeness, how did it feel to not get the closeness you wanted? If you wanted more distance, how did it feel to not get the distance you desired?

4. How did you feel when you left the room? When your spouse left the room?

5. What did you experience when you embraced?

6. When you were in the stationary position, how did you respond when you felt invaded?

7. How did you feel when you lacked control over the distance? Had control over the distance?

CHAPTER 2

Self

*If "I" give my love to you, what exactly am I giving and who
is the "I" making the offering, and who, by the way, are you?*
—Stephen Mitchell, Can Love Last?

God said to Moses, "I am who I am."
—Exodus 3:14

Who am I, and how do I fit into this marital relationship? This question about "I"—or the self—is crucial as we venture further into the mind and marriage. This sense of I, with feelings of who I am and how I want my spouse to see and relate to me, is associated with a concept called self studied by psychologists, neuroscientists, and Christian contemplatives. What is the self? How does it develop? What are its functions? What is its relationship to the mind and marriage? What problems can it create? These are the questions we will examine in this chapter.

The self is a part of the mind that allows us to see the activities or flow of the mind.[40] This understanding suggests that the mind not only has important functions such remembering, emoting, thinking, and deciding but that it is also able to observe and describe these mental activities. In actuality, the self is the only observer of the mind. No one else can see into your mind. Without the self, all the functions of the mind would be outside our awareness or in the dark. The self serves an important role of giving us a glimpse into our mind.

Barbara, a college professor, had the excellent ability of describing the flow of her mind. After an intense interchange with her husband, Mike, I asked her what she was experiencing. She replied, "I feel like little pins are being poked into my body. I can tell that I am breathing faster. I can tell that I am angry. Who wouldn't be? Look at how he talks down to me. I just want to say something that will make him feel small, the way he makes me feel."

Barbara's sense of being a witness to the experiences of her mind was providing her with a sense of knowing. This sense of knowing is a vital function of the self, according to Daniel Siegel.[41] How does this sense of knowing develop? It starts with a feeling in our body that ranges someplace between pleasure and pain, a feeling that is evoked from an interaction with another person. Antonio Damasio, a professor of neuroscience at the University of Southern California, refers to this quality as a primordial feeling.[42] Gerald May, a Christian psychiatrist and contemplative, recognizes this same physical response and refers to it as "raw, undifferentiated energy."[43] Barbara identified this primordial feeling as something like pins in her body.

Next, this initial physical reaction is followed by an emotional response. For example, a primordial feeling of pleasure may turn into an emotion of joy, whereas a raw feeling of pain may show up as anger. Because these physical and emotional responses are so tangible, they give us a feeling of knowing. Barbara had no doubts that what she felt was anger.

It is not enough for the self to observe and know these physical and emotional responses. To the mind, there must be a main character to whom these feelings are happening.[44] This main character—or protagonist—is the self. The self provides you with the sense that you are the one interacting and being affected by your spouse. In other words, the self provides us with a sense of ownership: "I am feeling uncomfortable," or "this is my anger." The experience feels very personal. It seems to be happening to "me."

As this sense of self observes and feels these physical and emotional reactions, it begins to tell a story of engagement with your spouse. In other words, the self becomes a narrator or author of your story. The self begins to create an account of how you felt before interacting with your spouse: "I was feeling fine until you got home." Then, it describes how you were altered by your encounter with your spouse: "After you ignored me, I felt sad and lonely." The self seems to sit back and observe these events and then put them into the form of a story.

I observed and listened as Barbara engaged in this narrative process. She told a story about how she normally felt: confident. However, interacting with Mike produced the opposite feeling: "small." Of course, this feeling was uncomfortable, so in response she began to feel angry. And the anger prepared her for action, for a fight. According to Barbara, she was preparing a way to get back at Mike, to back him into a corner. That part of her mind that we call the self was creating a story of physical sensations, emotional responses, perceptions, and a plan of action.

All of the functions of self—observing, knowing, owning, and telling a story—enable the self to speak with a voice of certainty. The self provides you with a sense that you are the only one observing and experiencing these feelings. You—and no one else—are in the position to describe how you felt before and after an interaction with your spouse. The utterance of the self is the singular voice in your head.

As the self creates this story, the account sounds not only certain but objective. We attribute this objectivity to a feeling of detachment from the event. It seems as if we have observed not only the interaction with our spouse, but also the functions of our mind from a distance. It is as if the self is viewing these external and internal events from a position of knowing, a faraway location, a place of objectivity. Therefore, as we tell our narrative, we tell it as if our view of the event is accurate. We come off sounding this way: "I am right."

We must acknowledge two developmental aspects of self as we enter marriage. The first is that the self has a long history. According to attachment theorists, the self that shows up in marital interactions began to take shape long ago in early relationships with our primary caregivers.[45] Therefore, the self is primed to feel, perceive, and respond in certain established patterns. A self that is secure is programmed to act in certain ways; likewise, bringing an insecure sense of self into marriage predisposes us to certain other ways of knowing, observing, and narrating our interactions. It is important for us to recognize and acknowledge this history of the self. By doing so, we can see how marital interactions reveal not only things about our spouse, but also characteristics of the self.

The second thing to recognize is that, prior to marriage, we were the clear author of our self: "This is who I am." But with marriage, our spouse becomes a "co-author" in this process of defining the self. In other words, our spouses now place their own views of who we are alongside our narratives. We become extremely invested in and sensitive to the accounts they tell about us because we most likely want them to be favorable. If our spouse creates positive narratives, we feel safe. However, unfavorable narratives feel dangerous to our sense of self, and as a result, the threat response is activated. Now, the self becomes protective and prepares for battle. According to Susan Johnson, a psychologist who developed Emotionally Focused Couple Therapy (EFT), how one spouse defines the other spouse is one of the keys to marital success.[46]

I observed this delicate process of co-authoring the story of self during one of my sessions with Kevin and Stephanie. Stephanie, a pharmaceutical representative, was describing Kevin as "angry, attacking, and unwilling to compromise." She continued her description of Kevin by saying that he failed to shoulder his share of the responsibility for raising the kids and running a family. Stephanie's account clearly did not fit Kevin's self narrative. Instead, he saw himself as responsible, patient, caring, and willing to negotiate.

Kevin's sense of self was threatened by the narrative being told by Stephanie, so what was he to do? He began the process of defending himself. He had to set the story straight because he viewed her account as inaccurate. Only by correcting the story, by telling a more accurate account, could he begin to feel safe again. For Kevin to feel close to Stephanie, their battle over stories had to be resolved. They had to bridge the gap between his story and hers.

The example of Kevin and Stephanie illustrates one of the problems associated with self—that is, battles over self definition—but there are other difficulties, according to Christian contemplatives, as well as scientists. Another problem connected with self is that the mind's natural tendency is to create a small self. Coming from a scientific perspective, Daniel Siegel writes, "My own reading of the neuroscience of self is that the cortex is naturally inclined to create a smaller and limited sense of self."[47] The implication is that the self has the potential for so much more but it confines itself to a limited range of functions.

Why do we have a small, or limited, sense of self? The explanation for this phenomenon is that the self can witness only a small fraction of the workings of the mind. Most of the mind is out of sight—in the unconscious—and therefore unrevealed to the self. In other words, the self has a narrow or "small" view of the mind, which results in a limited view of self.

Let me use an analogy to illustrate our restricted view of the mind. Suppose you are standing outside a room, looking in through a door that is slightly ajar. You can observe, know, and describe certain objects and activities in the room, but most of the contents of the room are out of your vision. Because of your angle, your view of the room is "small," or limited. You are grateful for your opportunity to look inside, but most of the room's contents are out of sight.

In the same way, the self is restricted in its ability to view the contents of the mind. It can be aware of certain bodily responses, emotional reactions, memories, and commentaries. However, if it concludes, "I am these thoughts and feelings," then it will be defining the self in a narrow way. In other words, it has the potential to be larger if it could witness additional physical sensations and mental properties, but at the present it is limited by what it observes.

I saw this notion played out in my session with Kevin and Stephanie. As his battle with Stephanie escalated, I saw Kevin move into an aggressive posture. Instead of defending himself, he began to attack Stephanie, pointing out her shortcomings. When she observed that he was getting nasty and angry, he denied both accusations. I think that many of his physical sensations, emotions, and behaviors were outside of his awareness. As a result, he had a limited or small perspective of himself. His self did include anger and nasty behavior, but he just could not see it. What else about Kevin was out of his view?

Another problem with the self is that it is often on prominent display. Instead of appearing small, the self now appears huge in our minds,[48] leading to the impression that there is only enough room in the relationship for what "I want, I feel, and I think." Finding out that our spouse has another opinion or desire can be very threatening. The self says, "There is not room for another point of view. Mine is correct. You must be wrong."

The strange thing about the self is that it can fluctuate between these two positions of being small and large. At times, the self can retreat to the background, less concerned about "my emotions, my opinions, and my needs." But, without notification, the self can become prominent, wanting its own way, following its own path, inflexible and unbending. Which self will show up? The answer to this question often determines the outcome of our marital interactions.

Besides putting itself on prominent display, the self also likes to be at the center of our lives.[49] In other words, it likes to be in charge and appears to be confident in its ability to direct our lives. It likes to declare, "I can clearly see what is going on; therefore, I know what needs to be done." However, according to the Christian contemplative Thomas Keating, the judgments made by the self are largely incorrect.[50] This view is echoed by neuroscientist Antonio Damasio:

Our only direct view of the mind depends on a part of that very mind, a self process that we have good reason to believe cannot provide a comprehensive and reliable account of what is going on. At first glance, after acknowledging the self as our entry into knowledge, it may appear paradoxical, not to mention ungrateful, to question its reliability.[51]

The final difficulty that the self presents is its tendency to separate itself from everyone else. The sense of self comes with the feeling that my body and my mind exist independently from others with whom I am interacting. The feelings in my body belong only to me and no one else. The contents of my mind—emotions, memories, narratives, and decisions to act—belong only to me and no one else. The self, because it observes, knows, and feels the event, gives us the sense that the event is happening only to us. However, both disciplines tell us that this sense of separation from others is simply an illusion.

The self is a necessary presence in the mind. Even though it provides us with only a glimpse of the mind, without the self, we would look like people sleepwalking. We would not be aware of, and neither could we describe, the contents and flow of the mind. This sense of self is a wonderful and indispensable part of the mind. It enables us to know physical sensations and mental functions such as emotions, memories, and thoughts. This awareness and feeling of knowing adds tremendous color and music to our lives.

However, there are also difficulties that the self can bring to our marriage. First of all, we can act self-assured. Instead of admitting that we have a limited view of what is happening both internally and interpersonally, we come across as if we are certain: "The way I see it is the right way." Also, the self can lead us into a self-centered frame of mind. What I think, I want, and I feel becomes paramount, discounting our spouse's needs, feelings, and perspective. We can also become self-protective. When we perceive that our spouse is defining us in a way that seems unpleasant and negative, we can rise up in defense of our self. Finally, we can become self-contained. We can experience our self as disconnected from our spouse, holding on to the belief that we are the only one being affected by the situation. All of these problems of the self—and mind—can spell problems for our marriage if they are not addressed properly.

Try this:

1. Notice your earliest reactions to an experience with your spouse today—your first impressions. Are they pleasant or unpleasant physical sensations? Can you describe them? Pay attention as the physical sensations turn into an emotion. Try to put a label on the feeling (e.g., anger, sadness, excitement, happiness).

2. Observe the story that you create in response to an interaction with your spouse today. What is your account of what happened?

3. After creating the story, ask yourself the following questions: Did it really happen the way my self wants to tell it? I wonder what my spouse's story of the event was? (Notice if you are open to another telling of the event.)

4. Take time to tell your story to your spouse. Now, reflect on these questions: Did you tell the story as if it was the "truth" about what happened? Or did you tell your story as if it was one perspective— but not the only one—of the event? Were you open to your spouse's story of the event?

5. Review your account again. Revisit a part of the story where you said something about your spouse. Now, leave your spouse out of the narrative. Rewrite that part of the story so that you describe the event in terms of what it says about you and your history.

CHAPTER 3

Body

Don't you know that your body is a temple of the Holy Spirit, who is in you?

—1 Corinthians 6:19

"It all depends on what you do with your body," said the trail guide. Many years ago I was on a trail ride where the instructor prepared us by covering "the basics" of body positioning. He claimed that our bodies were our most basic tool for controlling our horses while riding on the trail. Things like keeping your eyes up, looking ahead, keeping your back straight, and even having a relaxed face were all important when it came to sending messages to the horse. He said that he wanted us to feel relaxed and flexible. If we didn't have proper form and balance, the horse would feel it, and then the horse might stiffen his back and gait in response to our body position. Before this riding experience, it had never crossed my mind that, when it comes to riding, the body is the place to start.

Now, let's think about the rider and horse as an analogy for the body and mind. What if our mind is just as responsive to our body as the horse is to the rider's posture? What if our body is constantly communicating with our mind? What if the relaxation and flexibility of our body controls the balance and functioning of the mind? Could it be that the body is the place to start when it comes to understanding the mind?

Many neuroscientists, psychologists, and Christian contemplatives have made that claim. Antonio Damasio states that the body is the foundation of the mind.[52] This implies that the mind rests on and is affected by the stability of the body. Studies show the body functions well within a narrow range called homeostasis. However, the conditions of the body can easily fall outside this range, and when they do, the body becomes imbalanced. Now we are discovering that when the body gets out of the balance, the mind is sure to do the same.

Sitting with a couple in my office one day, Alex and Liz, I could see Liz's body changing right in front of me. A cloud seemed to come over her as she started looking at the floor, almost as if in trance. Her skin became pale and her body seemed to get smaller as she folded in upon herself. Tears were streaming down her cheeks. In a few brief moments, the exterior of Liz's body had completely changed. However, Alex was oblivious to these changes because he was not observing her body. As I discovered later, Liz was also not aware that her body had changed.

Looking to Christian contemplative thought, I decided that for Liz and Alex, their bodies were the place to start. According to Christian contemplatives, changing our mind rests upon greater awareness of and ability to calm our body. This seems to be the message that the Apostle Paul sent to the Christians in Corinth and Rome. Before telling the Christians in Rome to change their minds, he told them to present their bodies to God (Romans 12:1–2). To the Christians in Corinth, he told them to think of their bodies as temples. Now, to me, a temple is grand, prominent, and on display. You can't miss it! You shouldn't miss it! It is to be observed and treated with reverence. Christian contemplative John O'Donohue writes, "To spend time in silence before the mystery of your body brings you toward wisdom and holiness."[53] As I proceeded in my work with Liz and Alex, I wanted to help them slow down, observe, and respect the changes—or language—of their bodies.

Before examining something as complex as how our body responds to the behavior of our spouse, let's begin by examining something more simple: how the body communicates with the brain. The body is constantly monitoring and reporting to the brain about various systems within the body. For example, the body is paying attention to the amounts of CO_2 and oxygen in the body, pH levels, body temperature, and nutrients—sugars, fats, proteins—in circulation. The body then conveys this information directly to the brain through numerous chemical molecules.

What if these body chemistries fall outside of the body's needed and desired range? First, the brain detects and measures the physiological state of the body, looking for departures from the desired range. This happens unconsciously. Next, as mentioned previously, the body produces a feeling that ranges from pleasure to pain. When the internal chemistry falls within the desired range, we experience this as pleasure. However, we begin to feel discomfort when we depart from the narrow range of what is acceptable and become disturbed when we go for very long without addressing the situation. For example, when my stomach is empty, I experience stomach pangs and they don't stop until I satisfy my hunger. This second process of feeling pleasure and pain, unlike the first process, can become a conscious experience.

This examination of the body's process of maintaining an internal balance reveals some important physiological principles. First, the body is on the lookout for conditions that fall outside of the range of normal. Second, much of this process happens outside of our conscious awareness. Third, conditions that are identified as dangerous—things that threaten our safety—produce a feeling of unpleasantness or pain. And finally, the body, working with the mind, devises a response that attempts to remedy the situation and return us to a range of safety.

I was paying close attention to the messages being transmitted by Alex and Liz's bodies. After observing the shutting down of Liz's body, I turned to read Alex's body language. At that moment, he was talking faster and getting louder, and his posture had gotten stiff. I could tell that his breathing rate had accelerated and his skin tone had gotten redder. Obviously, Liz and Alex's external signals indicated vastly different bodily reactions. I could tell that their bodies were out of balance, and I wondered what was happening on the inside.

According to neuroscience, a small, almond-shaped set of neurons called the amygdala, located in the limbic area of the right hemisphere of the brain, picks up on incoming information that appears to threaten our safety. This structure makes a quick judgment about the danger of another person or situation. As long as we feel safe, we remain relaxed and available to our spouse. However, once the amygdala assesses that the situation is dangerous, the threat system is quickly activated. This detection of danger and our response occurs outside our conscious awareness. Before we are even aware of it, our body, brain, and mind are working to return us to safety.

Once the threat system is activated, our body moves out of balance.[54] Depending on how the amygdala assesses the danger, our body activates different branches of the autonomic nervous system, prompting the body to become either over-aroused or under-aroused. If our brain assesses that we are helpless and cannot do anything to protect our safety, the vagal branch of the parasympathetic nervous system is activated.[55] The vagal branch refers to the vagus nerve, the tenth of twelve cranial nerves. When this branch turns on, our heart rate is dramatically reduced, our digestion shuts down, we start sweating, and our speech is affected. This is called the freeze response. On the other hand, if our brain assesses that we can handle the danger, the sympathetic branch of the autonomic nervous system is activated.[56] When this happens, neurochemical and hormonal reactions occur, and we expend the energy that allows us to move and act. Our heart rate begins to accelerate as the body gets ready for action. Adrenaline as well as the stress hormone cortisol are released into the bloodstream. Our metabolism increases as we prepare for the energy demands that lie ahead. We are ready to fight or run away.

John Gottman, particularly concerned with the activation of the sympathetic branch, has conducted research on the relationship between hyper-arousal and marital satisfaction.[57] Many of his findings revolve around the connection between heart rate and marital happiness. Fast heart rates seem to be associated with a decline in marital happiness. When the heart rate exceeds 100 beats per minute (bpm), the activities of the sympathetic nervous system are engaged. Blood pressure increases, the liver and adrenal glands begin releasing fuels into the bloodstream, and fight-or-flight routines become more accessible. In his studies, he found that husbands who eventually divorced had heart rates 17 bpm higher than those in stable marriages. Gottman's research shows that interactions are better when our heart rate is well below 100 bpm.

As the body becomes aroused, important mental and interpersonal skills decline. There is a reduced ability to process information. As much as we want to listen, we just cannot do it. Since our spouse seems like the enemy, we lose our ability to be affectionate, to creatively problem-solve, and to be humorous. Instead, we become more defensive, we start repeating ourselves, we lose our ability to calm our bodies, we feel emotionally overwhelmed, and we are quick to fight or flee.

The bodies of Liz and Alex were out of balance in very disparate ways. Liz's body was responding to the interaction with hypo-arousal, whereas Alex's body was responding with hyper-arousal. If we could check in on their brains, we would see that the middle prefrontal cortex of both had shut down.[58] Without access to this region of the brain, Alex and Liz were unable to regulate their bodies and soothe their fears. Instead, caught up in a state of fight, Alex was prepared for battle, while Liz, frozen by fear, only wanted to shield herself from Alex's attack. Until their bodies relaxed, they were unable to bring about a change of mind that would bring love back into their relationship.

In this instance, Alex's mind in particular reminded me of a horse my daughter once rode. My daughter, ten years old at the time, was taking riding lessons, and this day she was riding a beautiful thoroughbred horse that had been a racehorse in her younger days. On other days, the horse had functioned superbly, obeying all of Elise's commands. However, this day was different. Something happened that caused her horse to bolt into a gallop. All she could do was hold on for dear life, because it was no longer under her control. Usually this horse was a magnificent thing to witness, but on this day she was out of control and it was terrifying. Fortunately, the trainer intervened quickly, the horse was brought under control, and my daughter was okay.

On another occasion, I was working with another couple, Ron and Natalie, when I observed discrepancies in the energy of their bodies and minds. The messages being sent by Natalie's body seemed to indicate hyper-arousal: stiff posture, loud voice, staring, and a red face. However, Ron looked much different. As Natalie was talking, he turned his body and face away from her, crossed his arms, and then seemed to quit listening. When I asked, "What is your body doing?" his response was, "What she said sounded like a put-down to me. I don't want to continue talking to her." He admitted that he felt hurt, he showed an awareness of how he had interpreted her message, and he acknowledged that he was in a self-protective mode. However, he seemed to have no awareness of his body.

Sometimes, I think we treat our bodies the way I treated the pizza delivery guy recently. His arrival with the pizza set into motion a series of events. Within minutes, my family and I were sitting at the table, eating the pizza, and engaged in a lively conversation. Thinking back on it, I hardly noticed the pizza delivery guy. What was he wearing? What expression did he have on his face? Where had he come from and where was he going? Unfortunately, I paid more attention to what was delivered than I did to the person who delivered it.

The body—think of it as the pizza delivery guy—arrives with important data about people and events. Then the mind, without hesitation, takes the input and acts upon it. The information provided by the body produces a cascade of mental functions: memories, emotions, narratives, and decisions to act. However, the delivery boy—that is, the body—gets ignored in the process. We often fail to stop and pay attention to the agent of the information. What is the body doing? How is the body feeling? What is it communicating?

If we stop to pay close attention to Ron's body and to the interaction between his body, brain, and mind from the perspective of a neuroscientist, what is happening? First, Ron's body received information about Natalie's tone of voice and facial expression. This data was transmitted to and received by the right hemisphere of Ron's brain. Research reveals that the right hemisphere is better at receiving information from the body than the left side of the brain.[59] As this information flowed up to the right limbic area, where the amygdala is located, the data was assessed: "Does this situation feel safe or dangerous?" In this situation, Ron's brain determined that the interaction with his wife was dangerous. The flow of information did not stop here. It continued to the right cortex, and then to the left cortex.[60] At this point, Ron began to make sense of the experience, as he put it into words. He started talking to me about his feelings, perceptions, and intentions. Unbeknownst to Ron, long before he put his experience into words, his mind had already created and implemented a plan of protection. This plan, which was out of Ron's consciousness, included the recall of memories, the arousal of emotions, the creation of a story, and a plan of action. His body was communicating all of these mental processes; however, neither he nor his wife was paying attention.

What do recent findings from neuroscience teach us about the body and the mind? First, we discover that most of the communications between the body and mind happen unconsciously. The body is communicating, but its message is often outside of our awareness. Second, research findings show that the body is communicating its reaction to an event long before we put our experience into words. However, the way the body communicates—with posture, tone of voice, and facial expression—is much more subtle than communication that comes in the form of language. Finally, neuroscience tells us that the body's wisdom about an event is much more accurate than the view that we describe with words.

The discoveries being made about the body-mind connection and the confidence placed in the wisdom of the body by neuroscience sounds very similar to the position taken by Christian contemplatives. Martin Laird, a Christian contemplative and professor of theology and religious studies at Villanova University writes, "The body is a great reservoir of wisdom."[61] Another Christian contemplative, John O'Donohue, captures the contemplative view in this way:

> The body is very truthful. You know from your own life that your body rarely lies. Your mind can deceive you and put all kinds of barriers between you and your nature; but your body does not lie. Your body tells you, if you attend to it, how your life is. . . . The body also has a wonderful intelligence. . . . It is unfortunate that often only when we are ill do we realize how tender, fragile, and precious is the house of belonging called the body.[62]

In these words, O'Donohue seems to be echoing an assertion by the Apostle Paul that our home on this earth is this body (2 Corinthians 5:6).

Spending time with this temple of the body is important to our minds and our marriages. If our body is out of balance, the mind will follow. If the body falls out of its narrow range of equilibrium, the mind will lean toward either chaos or rigidity. If the body is at low or high levels of energy, rather than in the middle, the mind is unable to access emotions, thoughts, and actions that foster satisfying relationships. The place to start is with our body. We must stop and listen to its intelligence. But it is only by slowing down and paying attention to the wisdom of body that we can retrain our mind and mend our marriage.

Try this:

1. Stop and spend five minutes in silence with your body today. Scan your body from your toes to the top of your head. Notice any pain or tension. Pay attention to any spots of tension and discomfort. Just allow your attention to rest on these areas and allow your body to relax.

2. Notice your body today when it is out of balance. Catch it before it springs into action. Now, instead of carrying out the planned behavior, just suspend the action. Pay attention to and describe your body. What is happening on the inside? Pay attention to your heart rate, breathing rate, and muscular tension. Now, what is happening on the outside? Describe your posture and facial expression.

3. Today, catch your body in the earliest stage of responding to a person or situation. At this stage, your body will simply feel pleasure or displeasure. Watch as your mind tries to make sense of this raw feeling. It will try to answer the following questions: What happened to cause this reaction? What emotion am I having? What am I going to do about it? Pay attention as your mind prepares your body to respond to the event.

CHAPTER 4

Memories

Marriage is a battleground for all of the unspoken,
underground streams that are brought together
underneath the steady flow of arrangements.
—*David Whyte, The Three Marriages*

The past is never dead. In fact, it's not even in the past.
—*William Faulkner, Requiem for a Nun*

All memories are not the same: they remind me of streams. Some flow above ground, are easy to see, and are within our awareness. "Aboveground" memories are the recollections we have of events from our past that we can recall with words. However, other memories are underground, out of sight, outside of awareness. Since we do not have knowledge of these memories, we are unable to put them into words. The bottom line is that in order to understand our mind and marriage, it is essential that we make sense of these repositories of the past.

Scientists have assigned names to these two types of memories: explicit and implicit. Explicit memories are the aboveground variety and are commonly ascribed to the left hemisphere of the brain, while implicit memories are underground and are encoded in the right side of the brain.[63]

These two types of memory not only reside in different parts of the brain, but they also exhibit unique characteristics. Let's start with explicit memories. First, they are clear. For example, remembering where you graduated from high school is an explicit memory because you have no doubt that this event happened on a specific day in your past. Second, this type of memory can be recalled with words. If someone asked you, you could tell them the name of your high school. Next, an explicit memory is recalled as having happened in the past.[64] When I recall my wedding, it seems obvious to me that this event happened in the past. This event has a clear timestamp on it: 1982. Finally, this type of memory clearly exists within conscious awareness.

Implicit memories are very different. The most important quality about this type of memory is that it happens outside of our awareness. The memory is activated, but we are often not knowledgeable of its presence. This leads to the second characteristic of implicit memories: They do not have a timestamp. When an implicit memory emerges, it does not show up as an event from the past. Instead, since the memory is operating outside of awareness, it seems as if we are reacting to something in the present moment. Next, implicit memories are wordless—of course, if you can't see the memory, you can't put it into words—they are communicated through body language. Only by being finely attuned to bodily sensations and emotions can we recognize the presence of implicit memories.

A recent conversation I had with Jason and Andrea, both in their forties, illustrates some of these characteristics of implicit memories. During the meeting, Andrea, a pharmaceutical representative, asked Jason, a real estate agent, what he wanted to do on their upcoming anniversary. To her surprise, Jason, who was usually very talkative, had no answer. Sitting there with a blank look on his face, Jason could not come up with a response to her question. Seeing signs of strong emotions, I knew that Andrea's question had hit a nerve.

Actually, Andrea's question had hit an implicit memory. Two weeks before their last anniversary, Jason had discovered that Andrea had

had an affair and he had insisted on a separation. As a result, they missed that anniversary. Since then, they had worked hard at restoring their marriage and now they were back together. But now, this question about their upcoming anniversary was colliding with Jason's implicit memories of their last one.

In an effort to understand Jason's behavior—that is, his inability to respond—I asked Jason to attend to his emotions and the physical sensations in his body. He began to describe the tension in his face and chest and the sick feeling in his stomach. This led him to identify a deep sense of sadness accompanied by frustration. It was only then, after tuning in to his body and emotions, that the memory of their last anniversary emerged into Jason's awareness. Now he understood the block. It was too painful to discuss their upcoming anniversary because of the sadness and anger attached to their last one.

Let's return to the notion that beneath conscious memories are unconscious ones, an idea that is accepted by both scientists and Christian contemplatives. Who proposed this idea that much of the mind operates outside of our awareness? Scientists credit Sigmund Freud with airing this idea a century ago.[65] However, centuries before Freud, Christian contemplatives such as John of the Cross—from the sixteenth century—had a profound appreciation for the active life of the mind that was flowing outside of awareness.[66] John of the Cross, when referring to what is now called the unconscious, used the term "darkness." This term implies that there are activities of the mind—such as memory—that take place in hidden ways, outside of our conscious control. These functions of the mind happen mysteriously, in secret, in the dark.

This was clearly the case with Jason. At first, he was not aware of his memories from his last anniversary, but they were making themselves known in both subtle and not-so-subtle ways. The changes in his body language—a redder skin tone, frowning, and a shift in posture—were subtle, but his lack of speech was apparent to everyone. In contrast, Jason's memories of the past were evident to no one. It was only after tuning in to his physical sensations and emotions that these memories came out of the dark into conscious awareness.

For a while, Jason's implicit memories were not only operating in the dark, they were also exerting tremendous power over his body, emotions, and behavior. The notion that the unconscious has tremendous power—greater than that of the conscious mind—is an idea upon which scientists and Christian contemplatives agree. According to Marion Solomon and Stan Tatkin, leaders in the field of marriage counseling, interactions among marriage partners are primarily shaped and controlled by unconscious systems.[67] They claim that more than 90 percent of what is happening between spouses—including memories—is occurring at this unconscious level. Christian contemplative Richard Rohr uses a similar percentage.[68] He claims that 95 percent of our reactions to others come out of the unconscious dimension of the mind.

The unconscious level seems to be the dimension in which our marriage swims, so let's focus our attention on unconscious, implicit memories. First, where do they originate? According to both science and centering prayer, the tributaries of implicit memories are all the emotionally laden events of our past, from birth to recent history.[69] Research from neuroscience indicates that implicit memories go back to our earliest years, especially to the first eighteen months of our lives. Many researchers believe that only implicit memories—not explicit ones—are being recorded during these beginning months.[70] Of course, without language skills, we cannot put our earliest memories into words, but they are nonetheless being stored away for future reference. Our mind and memory are paying particular attention to our initial interactions with the significant people in our lives. The blueprints that are established—called attachment patterns—are being stored away in the implicit memory. And if these templates are fear-provoking, implicit memories will create expectations of how life will unfold in the future.

On top of this foundational level, all of the emotionally laden episodes from our past continue to be laid down in the form of implicit memories. Fear-evoking experiences are often not recorded and stored in conscious memory, but they are never missed by the unconscious memory process. When anything scary happens, implicit memory records the sights and sounds of the event and then files them away as signs of danger.[71] From then on, any time you encounter a similar circumstance, unconscious memory reminds you—outside of your knowledge—of the dangerous past occasion.

This process clearly happened with Jason. The talk of the next anniversary brought up implicit memories of his last one. His memory of the past was full of unpleasant sights, sounds, and sensations, and now those memories were creating expectations for his next anniversary. Outside of Jason's awareness, his implicit memories were reminding him of the connection between the past and the future, and they were trying to protect him from another bad experience.

It is vital to our marriage to understand and recognize when implicit memories are intruding into the present. Of course, we all carry around painful memories of past hurts. As John O'Donohue says, "There is no one who is not damaged internally in some way."[72] Psychologist John Gottman expresses the same view: "No one escapes childhood without some scars."[73] And when we carry wounds from childhood, current interactions with our spouse can remind us of the past. When this happens, implicit memories from our earliest relationships are triggered. Current interactions can remind us of early attachment failures. Now we are getting to the sources of the underground stream.

During one of our sessions, I helped Macie and Will get to the implicit root of a frustrating series of events. Their falling out began during a weekend visit by some of Will's relatives. According to Macie, Will seemed to turn all of his attention to his visiting relatives and totally forgot about her. She perceived that he was soaking in and enjoying all the attention they gave him in return, oblivious to her need for just a little bit of his consideration. She could feel herself getting more and more despondent but she was determined not to show it. Nevertheless, she noticed that she was becoming more withdrawn as the weekend progressed.

Macie admitted that her behavior seemed like an overreaction, so we decided to explore connections between the unpleasant weekend and implicit memories from her past. Macie began to draw parallels between childhood experiences and the recent events. She remembered feeling left out as a child when her family spent time with relatives. During these temporary stays, her parents ignored her the same way that Will had. These childhood visits were special for her parents but not for Macie. Her parents were so focused on their relatives that she wound up feeling lonely and alone. Now, where she had been unable to make the connections before, she was beginning to see how current events were reminding her of old experiences. Her unconscious had attached feelings from her childhood to her interactions with Will. The conversation between Macie and I allowed her to see how the past had intruded into the present.

One of our difficulties in recognizing implicit memories is that they do not have a timestamp. Wouldn't it be nice if, when we find ourselves reacting to our spouse, we could stop and say, "I am responding in this way to this event because it reminds me of something that happened when I was a child"? But because we are dealing with memories that are outside of awareness, it appears as if the present event is triggering our intense response. Without this ability to say "this feeling is related to my past," we assign the source of our misery to our spouse, in the same way that Macie did.[74] We sense that our spouse is hurting us, and all the while, implicit memories of old hurts are outside of our awareness.

How do implicit memories intrude into the present? Neuroscience tells us that all the information we receive from our spouse passes through the right limbic area of the brain, beginning with the amygdala, which is home to our deepest implicit memories.[75] The right side of the amygdala quickly receives the data and makes important judgments about whether the new information constitutes a threat or not. In a matter of milliseconds, the threat response system can be mobilized if the present interchange reminds us of implicit memories of past, hurtful interactions.[76] Once this self-protective system is activated, the implicit memories can then influence our perceptions and experience of the current event. Remember how Macie perceived that Will was oblivious to her need for attention. To Macie, it seemed as if Will only cared about his relatives, not her. These perceptions of Will arose because they fit with Macie's implicit memories of the past.

Have you ever seen an underground stream erupt as a geyser? The geyser, with all of its power, steam, and beauty is noticed by everyone. Unlike geysers, however, when an underground stream of implicit memories bursts upon the scene, it often goes unnoticed. The signals of implicit memories are very specific—powerful bodily sensations and surges of strong emotions—but they can be missed. For example, we may experience a sudden rush of adrenaline or the tightening of muscles. Or, sensing that we are out of balance, we may feel flooded with emotions that push us toward either chaos (too much emotion) or rigidity (emotional deadness). However, instead of recognizing these physical and emotional signals for what they are—that is, indicators of implicit memories—we misinterpret them as reactions to the present situation. Failing to see that our response is out of proportion to the circumstances, we may remain convinced that our behavior is tied to events that we have knowledge of, as opposed to memories outside of our awareness.

Fortunately, for Macie and Will, they were able to draw connections between recent circumstances and Macie's implicit memories. She uncovered the root of her reactions to weekend events; that is, experiences from her past. Now, instead of blaming Will for rude and inconsiderate behavior, she saw how episodes from the past were shaping her perceptions of the present. And instead of being trapped in painful emotions and unhelpful behaviors—feeling lonely and acting withdrawn—she was now free to engage in more loving behavior with her husband.

In this example, Macie escaped the past. However, both scientific and Christian contemplative thinkers assert that implicit memories from the past often imprison us. Jumping from the past into the present, they control our reactions to our spouse, all the while outside of our awareness. This is the worst of all prisons. We are confined but don't even see the walls that restrict our freedom.

The implicit realm of memory is at the very core of marriage.[77] By recognizing the signals of our unconscious memories, we have the opportunity to bring them into conscious awareness. And by attending to their meaning, by understanding them, we can change the impact that these memories have upon our marital interactions. Finally, we can begin to live in the present and leave our past where it belongs—in the past.

Try this:

1. Since we often rationalize our reactions to situations—and fail to see that our behaviors are out of proportion to the event—simply notice a "strong" physical or emotional response to an interaction with your spouse. Stop to describe your physical and emotional reaction. Entertain the possibility that your behavior may be tied to memories from your past—and not just to the current circumstance. Pause and ask yourself these questions: Is this interaction similar to an early childhood experience? Am I being treated in a way that seems reminiscent of treatment I received as a child?

2. One of our goals is to bring implicit memories into conscious awareness. Try to verbally describe how early relationships may have failed to meet your needs for security. Developing a narrative helps you make more sense out of your life and allows you to live more fully in the present.

3. Once you have developed a narrative of your early attachment relationships, it can be helpful to juxtapose your memory with a dis-

confirming present experience.[78] *For example, suppose your child-hood memory is of a parent who failed to take you seriously. Now, with this memory in mind, pay attention to a present interaction with your spouse in which your spouse does the opposite of your parent. That is, catch yourself in an interchange with your spouse in which your spouse is taking you seriously.*

CHAPTER 5

Emotions

At the root of all war is fear.
—*Thomas Merton, New Seeds of Contemplation*

When the weave of affection starts to unravel
And anger begins to sear the ground between you,
Before this weather of grief invites
The black seed of bitterness to find root,
May your souls come to kiss.
—*John O'Donohue, "For Love in a Time of Conflict"*

As John O'Donohue's poem "For Love in a Time of Conflict" suggests, love does not quickly fall apart. Instead, it slowly unravels, like the strands of a rope that have been yanked at by restless hands over a long period of time. And as love becomes undone, a relationship that was once filled with affection slowly turns into an ugly war, sometimes scorching and at other times freezing the connection between spouses. As Thomas Merton, a Christian contemplative, points out, at the root of this war is fear. In order to end—or even better, prevent—this destructive fight, we must understand how fear lives and flows within us. How does fear take root and grow? How does it gain hold of the mind and push us around? And how does it begin to outwit love that once seemed so resistant to threats? In this chapter, we will examine scientific and Christian contemplative responses to these questions.

Both science and Centering Prayer agree that fear is our most basic response when something happens to undermine our need for security.[79] This intense need for a secure connection appears within the first days of our life and continues into our adult marital relationship. Nothing seems to rival this need to feel safe, warm, nurtured, and attended to by the person we love. But when we feel that we are unwanted or excluded, our threat protection system is activated.

The threat protection system easily and quickly activates threat-based emotions. The two most powerful ones are anger and fear.[80] According to Paul Gilbert, a British psychologist, anger is simply another face of fear. Anger may seem confident, bold, and self-assured, but underneath all the bravado rests a fear of being hurt, of losing control, or of being marginalized, ignored, or isolated. Researchers claim that we have only a few key fears. And the ones that we are most commonly preoccupied with are related to being shamed, criticized, rejected, and left unwanted.

These were the types of emotions being described in my office one day by Robby and Monica. They both acknowledged that Robby, a building contractor, was often filled with anger and resentment toward Monica. Sometimes the event that triggered the anger could be identified, but oftentimes it seemed to just come out of the blue. And once it appeared, the anger was vicious. Robby seemed to be on the verge of losing control, and it scared both of them. But what was feeding all of this anger?

Neuroscience is interested in this question of how the threat protection system gets activated. According to brain research, the information we receive from our spouse passes through the right limbic area of the brain, beginning with the amygdala. In small fractions of a second, the amygdala asks and answers the most basic question: Is this good or is this bad? In other words, the amygdala is determining if the interaction with your spouse is providing you with the safety and security that you desperately desire. If the signs of safety are missing, the amygdala may tag the interaction with a warning: "Be afraid. Be very afraid."[81]

Once an interaction is perceived by the amygdala as a threat, fear is activated, along with a physical chain reaction.[82] First, the amygdala dispatches commands to the hypothalamus and the brain stem that results in several physical responses. The heart rate accelerates, the respiration rate increases, and the gut contracts. Cortisol is secreted into the blood, and the muscles in the face adopt a look of alarm. Fear quickly alters chemistries in the body and causes smooth muscles in the internal organs to contract or dilate. At the same time, the middle prefrontal cortex of the brain is being shut off by the scared amygdala. As these physiological responses occur, the mind is taking notice and labeling these physical reactions as "fear." According to neuroscientist Antonio Damasio, fear is actually this perception of bodily sensations.

The physical sensations of fear were difficult, but not impossible, for Robby to identify. One day, Monica and Robby were sitting in my office when the anger appeared. I asked him to describe the physical sensations associated with the anger. The first thing he noticed was tension in his chest. Next, he became aware of his shortness of breath. Finally, he observed muscular tension in his hands and arms. "I feel like striking out at something but it feels like my arms are tied," he remarked. His ability to control this impulse to hit provided me with a sense of safety for them. Still, we wondered what was at the root of his anger— or fear.

Fear can be triggered by either events that are happening at the moment or by events that have happened in the past, by memories.[83] Of course, harsh criticism, verbal abuse, or a cold shoulder can feel threatening to our sense of security. The event happens in the present, we are aware that it seems threatening, and we can connect the event with the feeling of fear. However, at other times, the present event is perceived through the filter of unconscious, implicit memories. As information about a present interaction enters the amygdala, it gets washed with implicit memories, also stored in the amygdala. As a result, if the present interaction reminds us of a fear-provoking past event, we may respond to the current situation with the same fear with which we responded to an earlier—outside of awareness—event. We may think that we are afraid of the current event, but we are actually responding in fear to an earlier episode.

In Robby's case, he typically perceived himself as responding to Monica's hurtful behavior—she was the culprit—but with time, he became aware that Monica's behavior was simply a reminder of his mother's terrifying behavior. When he was a child, his mother's alcoholism led her to frequently engage in unpredictable, egotistical, and threatening behavior. Sometimes, his mother would sit him down and make unkind, untrue accusations against him. As a small child, what could he do? He was filled with justifiable rage, but his dad instructed him to act compliant until his mother ran out of steam. Robby found it best just to stay away from his mother as much as possible.

Not only was Robby responding to unconscious memories from his past, but fear was also guiding his perceptions of the present. According to scientific research, when fear takes over our perceptions, it can focus our attention on the most threatening aspect of an experience.[84] In Robby's case, he was extremely alert to any of Monica's behavior that could be considered out of the ordinary, conceited, or accusatory—no matter how minor or inconsequential. In an attempt to protect him, Robby's mind focused on these signs of danger, ignoring information that might contradict his quick perceptions, conclusions, and reactions. As John O'Donohue says, looking at our marriage through fearful eyes causes us to see only the things that can damage or threaten us.[85]

From our preceding discussion of the relationship between fear, the body, implicit memories, and perceptions, it becomes obvious that fear is primarily an unconscious process. This characteristic of fear is acknowledged by both Christian contemplative and scientific thinkers. According to psychologist Louis Cozolino, outside of our awareness, fear is evaluating and producing responses to information long before these experiences emerge into awareness.[86] Unconsciously, the emotion of fear is cooperating with the body, memories, and perceptions to produce a protective response to a threatening situation.

This was clearly the case for Robby. Fear had produced a predictable cascade of events. It had activated unconscious memories from childhood, produced strong physical sensations, and finally caused him to focus on the most threatening aspects of his interactions with Monica. Now, as an adult, he no longer felt compelled to cower in fear from a threatening mother figure. Instead, with the assistance of fear, he was ready to confront Monica with anger. And throughout the process, all of these reactions were happening outside of Robby's awareness.

As the example of Robby illustrates, when the emotion of fear is activated we are flooded with emotions that can overwhelm our mind. Attachment theorists use attachment styles to help us understand two basic strategies for trying to regulate this sense of being overwhelmed with fear.[87] The first strategy, defined as anxious, refers to a tendency to under-regulate emotions, while the second strategy, referred to as avoidant, refers to a tendency to over-regulate emotions. If you employ the first approach, you probably reach out to others and express your emotions when you feel overwhelmed. On the other hand, if you use the second approach, you are more apt to turn inward and avoid talking to others about your feelings. Avoidant people are less attentive to emotions and accompanying physical sensations, while anxious people rivet their attention on emotions and physical sensations.

Robby clearly had learned and now employed an anxious strategy. When Robby's behavior activated his threat response system, he was quick to express the emotion that he was most aware of: anger. However, the problem was that he went overboard and unleashed the anger onto Monica. Underneath his expression of emotion, he was looking for signs of safety from Monica—that she was not like his mother—but Monica could not see below the surface. Instead, the intensity of Robby's emotional expression activated Monica's own protective system. Her strategy was to withdraw, so the reassurance that Robby so desired went unfulfilled. Robby leaned in one direction—toward under-regulating his emotions—while Monica leaned in the opposite direction—toward over-regulating her emotions.

Just like Monica and Robby, in spite of our efforts to regulate our fear, we often feel overwhelmed with emotions. We get out of balance and experience either too much or too little emotional energy.[88] In other words, we can become either too aroused and our minds become chaotic, or we have too little emotional energy and become stuck in rigidity. Imagine a marriage between two highly aroused partners. They cannot regulate their emotions and they both accelerate into intense emotions at the drop of a hat. On the other hand, if two low energy people are married to each other, they will often avoid talking to each other about their emotions. Instead, they will turn inward for solace after a fear-provoking experience.

What are we supposed to do with unregulated fear? According to Christian contemplative Richard Rohr, "Be not afraid" is the most common single line in the Bible.[89] Have you ever wondered why this command is so common? Neuroscience offers us two possible explanations. According to Louis Cozolino, fear actually outranks and outwits love in several ways.[90] Operating from the right, subcortical regions of the brain, fear is faster, automatic, and unconscious. Love, which seems to operate out of the middle prefrontal cortex, is a slower, more conscious process. Neurobiologically, when fear is activated, it turns off the middle prefrontal cortex.

This leads to a second neurobiological explanation for not being afraid.[91] Recent findings suggest that the mind works in terms of patterns. This simply means that if one system is turned on, then another one will be turned off, like a light switch. In terms of emotional patterns, if you are anxious, you cannot also be relaxed. One system negates the other system. In the same way, if you are afraid, this will block feelings of love. You can't feel frightened and affectionate at the same time.

Robby wanted to have a loving response to his wife, but fear was blocking access to this part of his mind. Through marital therapy, we were beginning to reverse his mental patterns so that he could operate more out of love. Several strategies helped. Tuning in to and labeling his emotions and physical sensations helped him calm down the firing of the amygdala. Bringing implicit memories into conscious awareness helped him disconnect the past from the present. And increasing his awareness of mental functions led him to question his fear-provoking perceptions. Slowly but surely, he was moving from fear to love.

It behooves us to "be not afraid." Keeping fear within balance allows our mind to support the well-being of our marriage. However, fear is a powerful emotion, one which has the tendency to easily and quickly take over the functions of the mind. We have seen in this chapter that this reaction is completely understandable because emotions involve the body; they are linked to memories, they alter our perceptions, and they operate unconsciously. According to Thomas Keating, we will continue to be pushed around by fear if the unconscious is unchanged.[92] I would add that the entire emotional program needs to be revamped—bodily awareness, implicit memories, perceptions, and the unconscious—in order to tame this function of the mind. By learning to regulate our fear, we can bring peace back into our marriage, and return love to the center of our relationship.

Try this:

1. If you feel angry at your spouse today, stop and ask yourself: "Is some type of fear hiding behind the anger?" Look for a fear of losing control, of being hurt, of being ignored, or of being criticized.

2. The next time you feel afraid (or angry), focus on the physical sensations of the emotion. How does it feel in your body? Put words to how you are feeling in your body. Notice the effects of putting your physical reaction into words.

3. Notice an interaction with your spouse that triggers your threat response system. After identifying and describing the event, ask your-

self: "How is this event similar to childhood interactions with my family?" First, entertain the possibility that there are similarities. Then look closely for similarities.

4. When you experience a threat-based emotion, notice your strategy for regulating it. Do you reach out to others for support or do you turn inward? Is the emotion obvious to all or do you tend to bottle it inside? It's important to identify your natural pattern.

CHAPTER 6

Narratives

There's a fiction in the space between
You and me
A fabrication of a grand scheme
Where I am the scary monster
   —Tracy Chapman, "Telling Stories"

I am always at a loss to know how much
 to believe of my own stories.
   —Washington Irving, Tales of a Traveler

There is a gap between spouses, and that space is filled with stories. These narratives will probably determine whether our marriage succeeds or fails. Stories come in many varieties. Many are about ourselves, others are accounts of our spouse, and some are about our marital relationship. These narratives are our attempts to explain events and feelings. Stories are our best efforts to make sense out of the interactions that take place between us. We can't help but weave these yarns! As writer Diane Ackerman says, "Born fictioneers, all of us, we quest for causes and explanations."[93] And these narratives that we author are at the center of our marriage. For that reason, it is vital that we understand them.

Narratives are another one of the mind's mechanisms for organizing information. However, long before this narrative process gets activated, the right hemisphere of the brain has already begun organizing incoming data. The information we receive from our spouse first enters and passes through the right hemisphere of the brain. As mentioned in previous chapters, this operation starts as data enters the right limbic area of the brain, beginning with the amygdala. The amygdala, in its efforts to protect us, looks for signs of trouble, and if signs of safety are missing, the amygdala sends commands to the brain stem that results in the activation of several physical responses. Additionally, as information about the present event enters the amygdala, it gets immersed in implicit memories, also stored in the amygdala. During this soaking process, present interactions can remind us of and bring up past memories of fear-evoking events. At the same time, the middle prefrontal cortex of the brain is being shut off by the scared amygdala. All the while, this right brain process happens outside of our awareness.

Let me illustrate this process by telling you about a recent conversation I had with Alisha, who worked in a call center, and Justin, a land surveyor employed by the city. The beginning of Justin's story was very simple: "All I did was ask her to not use the credit card." However, Alisha had a very different version of events. She said, "When he approached me, I knew that something was wrong. He looked uptight and nervous." Alisha's story zeroed in on the movement in Justin's right brain, actions unbeknownst to him. What were these activities? According to my understanding, outside of his awareness, Justin was remembering other straightforward requests that he had made of his wife. And along with these past memories, he was probably feeling anxious as he prepared for another convoluted, confusing, and antagonistic conversation. According to brain research, all of this right brain information was organized before he uttered the first line of his story.

It is only as information moves up to the right cortex and then into the left cortex that narratives begin to form. Here, in the left cortex, the language centers reside. With the raw material—bodily sensations, emotions, and memories—that the right side provides, the left brain begins to create a story.[94] Knowledge that once existed in the darkness of the right brain now begins to take shape in conscious awareness and in words. As Antonio Damasio says, "Whatever plays in the nonverbal tracks of our minds is rapidly translated into words and sentences."[95]

According to both Christian contemplative and scientific thinkers, our narratives are limited by the raw material that the left hemisphere receives from the right side. According to Thomas Keating, our commentaries are attached to and support our emotions and memories.[96] Before we even know it, the language centers of the left brain are forming a story that explains what we are feeling and the cause of that emotion. Outside of our awareness, the present event is being washed in memories from the past. This entire process happens quickly, in secret, before a narrative emerges into our conscious awareness.

After listening to Justin and Alisha's disparate accounts of their painful interaction, I suggested to them, "You know, our version of events can often get quite skewed. Can we just accept that both of you told it the way you remembered it? Perhaps we don't need to argue over whose story is right." I have said something similar on many occasions, and couples usually go along with my request. Not Justin. "No, it happened the way I said it did. Alisha is lying," he declared. I was at a loss as to what to say next.

According to discoveries emerging from neuroscience, Justin's response is quite understandable, because once a narrative emerges, it seems factual and we sound certain as we recount our story of the event. According to neuroscientist Andrew Newberg, "We are all biased toward perceiving our own beliefs as true."[97] What makes us so sure that our story contains the truth? According to Mark Leary, Professor of Psychology at Duke University, this bias occurs because we cannot step outside ourselves to view our spouse, our marriage, or ourselves in an impartial fashion.[98] As a result, we can only see things from one viewpoint: our own. With only one "legitimate" viewpoint to draw from, we process information in a one-sided manner, leading us to believe that we see things accurately.

Second, we must remember that our story has an author—ourselves.

We are the one observing our spouse, our marriage, and ourselves, and this sense of seeing brings with it a sense of proprietorship. Once we put what we are observing into words—into a story—we take ownership of it. It is now *my* story. Antonio Damasio proposes that this sensation of ownership evokes a feeling of truth.[99] A sense of proprietorship engenders an impression of rightness. We wind up thinking and sounding this way: "The way I view it is correct."

We may fall into the trap of believing that our narratives are true, but scientists and Christian contemplatives are telling us that our narratives are selective. As John O'Donohue says, "The story is rarely presented for what it is: a selective version."[100] What does this mean? It means that narratives make sense of events based upon minimal amounts of information. A story can contain only a small portion of the experiences in our marriage, and the mind selects only the details that it believes are significant. Those particulars that support our emotions and memories are allowed into the story, while everything else is excluded.

The fact that the left brain depends on information flowing from the right to create a story also accounts for the selective nature of stories.[101] The left brain can only put into words and sentences what it receives from the right side, but there are often interferences with the transfer of information. Perhaps we are not even paying attention to the flow of energy and information from the right side. If that's the case, then we may not notice physical and emotional sensations. When the left mode has an impoverished flow of knowledge from the right side, then, according to research from neuroscience, the left side will simply make something up. Antonio Damasio puts it this way, "The creative languaged mind is prone to indulge in fiction. The left cerebral hemisphere of humans is prone to fabricating verbal narratives that do not necessarily accord with the truth."[102]

I had an idea that Justin was indulging in some fiction. He said: "When I made my request of Alisha, I was feeling as calm as I am right now." Reading his body language, he did not appear relaxed as he was telling me this, and according to Alisha, he had not been in a calm state before. Justin did not have a history of paying close attention to the raw material of his right brain. Therefore, I assumed that he was just making up the "I was calm" part of his story.

In keeping with our focus upon the threat response system of the mind, how is the narrative process affected when our security and sense of connection to our spouse is being jeopardized? What if our spouse has just said something unkind, looked the other way, or been insensitive to our needs? When we feel pushed away, undesired, or unwanted by our spouse, our mind begins to develop stories that defend and protect. If feelings of anger emerge, we create a narrative that justifies this initial response. On the other hand, when we experience fear, we weave a story with information that supports this reaction. As Daniel Bennett, Professor of Philosophy at Tufts University, says, "Our fundamental tactic of self-protection . . . is not spinning webs or building dams [as spiders and beavers do], but telling stories."[103]

My assumption was that Alisha and Justin were both using stories for self-protection. Justin was afraid that Alisha, who had a history of telling lies, would mislead him once again, so he needed a story that was full of truth. "I'm sure I remember it the way it happened, but Alisha only tells lies," he declared. On the other hand, Alisha's greatest fear was of "being small" so she needed a story that would shake Justin's position of power and enhance her own importance. "I told him that he has more trouble controlling his spending than I do," she reported.

The self-protective nature of narratives can distract us from our real fear and vulnerabilities. The husband presents an account that shields him against any responsibility or blame for the problem. At the same time, the wife tells a story that defends her from any shame or guilt. Since these narratives emerge from the logical, left brain, they may seem perfectly reasonable to the teller of the story. However, vulnerable feelings of disconnection and fear may remain out of consciousness and out of their stories all the while. As Stan Tatkin, the originator of the Psychobiological Approach to Couple Therapy (PACT), says,

"When couples seek therapy for their relationships, their conscious narratives of what is wrong rarely touch the underlying defensive-protective dynamic that may be causing problems between them."[104] In other words, our stories are often a misleading account of what we really feel.

What if Alisha and Justin's narratives had addressed the truth of how they really felt? How would this have altered their stories? I imagine Alisha's account sounding like this: "It hurts so badly that you have such a low estimation of me. I am afraid that you will eventually give up on me and leave. I just want you to think well of me and have some confidence in me." On the other hand, I envision Justin telling this story: "I am afraid of being in the dark. It scares me to think that you might not be honest with me. I just want you to include me in your planning." But Alisha and Justin were not ready to be this honest with each other. As a result, their narratives distracted them from stories that would help repair their relationship.

This reminds me of something I once read in *Love and War in Intimate Relationships*: that a story can be a "red herring"—something that is intended to divert attention from the problem at hand. This expression has been thought to originate from a technique for training young scent hounds. Apparently, the red herring—a fish cured in brine or heavily smoked, giving the fish a strong smell—would be dragged along a path until a puppy learned to follow the trail. Later, when the dog was being trained to follow the faint odor of a fox, the trainer would teach the dog to follow the weak scent rather than the strong stench of the red herring. Our challenge is to follow the fainter scent of truth rather than the strong smell of our stories.

The idea of not going after our story is difficult because, to us, our narratives are true. But why are we so quick to accept this illusion that our story is accurate? I'm sure you have heard the phrase, the least experienced fisherman always catches the biggest fish. The truth is that our own narratives are just "fish stories." In spite of our best efforts, they are probably a long way from what really happened. They are usually red herrings that detract us from deeper issues, issues that can bring us closer together.

So far, we have been focusing on *what* is said; but *how* we say it is equally as important. Psychology research reveals that the way we tell our narrative is affected by our attachment style.[105] People with insecure attachment patterns are apt to tell stories that are hard to follow. For example, a person in an avoidant state of mind gives an extremely brief account. They tell us little, and often contradict themselves, making their stories difficult to relate to. On the other hand, someone in an anxious state of mind provides us with an overly lengthy tale. Their narratives overwhelm us with extraneous details, and events from the past keep intruding into the story. By the end of their account, we may feel totally confused.

This discussion points us toward the social nature of storytelling. A narrative is an activity between two people: the teller and the listener. To construct helpful stories, each person has an important role. The teller must provide a truthful, succinct, relevant, and clear account, while the listener must give focused attention and listen actively. Under these conditions, they can develop shared narratives, stories that have the ring of truth to both partners.

I try to imagine Alisha and Justin's shared story. I suppose it would go something like this: "We want to work together on our finances. This means that we will treat each other as equals. In other words, we will share power when it comes to managing money. We must have confidence that the other person is doing what they say they are doing and that they are looking out for the welfare of the family. In all things, we want to be respectful of and respected by the other person."

When this cooperative spirit breaks down, we wind up with *his* and *her* stories. Instead of narratives bringing us together, we can find ourselves in separate corners. He has his version of events—which he considers to be "the truth"—while she has her own separate account of what happened—which she also attests to be accurate. As they drift apart in this storytelling process, the stories have a tendency to become increasingly negative. The other person and their marriage is more often than not cast in a negative light. As John Gottman, the developer of Gottman Method Couples Therapy, reports, "If switched to a negative story-of-us, the relationship will almost certainly follow a sad, predictable trajectory."[106]

This process of weaving negative stories can create a vicious cycle. When we hear our spouse tell an antagonistic tale about our marriage, or us, it triggers our threat response system. Then, the cascade of mental processes in the right brain—the recognition of physical sensations, the triggering of old memories, and the flow of strong emotions—provides us with the raw materials we need for our own narratives. Our stories, birthed in fear, are prone to be defensive, reactive, and attacking. Then, we find ourselves mimicking our spouse. That is, we also wind up creating adverse accounts about our spouse and marriage. The future of the marriage does not look promising under these storytelling conditions.

Things did not look good for Alisha and Justin this day in my office. They were caught in a vicious cycle. They were each telling negative stories about the other and it seemed as if there was no way out. Her stories threatened him, so he created a self-protective and attacking narrative. Then, because she was so afraid, she devised a story that was equally as argumentative. They were moving away from stories that could help as they followed the pull of these negative and unproductive stories.

What we want are stories that remind us of truth. Christian contemplatives point us toward an ancient fisherman who was also known for his storytelling abilities: Jesus. He was known for telling the truth. He was also famous for employing a unique storytelling technique: the use of parables. A *parable* is defined as a metaphor or simile drawn from nature or common life. According to Thomas Keating, the contemplative practice of Centering Prayer is patterned on a parable given by Jesus. In this parable, Jesus taught that prayer was like going into a room, closing the door, and talking to God in secret (Matthew 6:6).[107]

According to Keating, by staying in our inner room—contemplative prayer—we become willing to let go of our illusion that the way we see our spouse, our marriage, and ourselves is accurate.

Neuroscience experts and Christian contemplatives are saying that contemplative practice is a way out of negative, unproductive stories, narratives that are often referred to as "prisons." Daniel Siegel says, "Our ordinary language can be a prison, locking us in the jail of our own redundancies, dulling our senses, clouding our focus."[108] It seems counterintuitive that going into one room—an inner room of contemplative prayer—can release us from another compartment—the prison of our old narratives—but once we are released from the prison of our old narratives, we are enabled to create new stories of our spouse, our marriage, and ourselves.

The creation of new stories is at the core of narrative therapy, a contemporary form of marriage counseling. Gene Freedman and Jill Combs, leaders in narrative couple therapy, argue that alternative stories can enable us to live out new identities, new marriages, and new futures.[109] This process of moving from old to new narratives begins by telling stories of truth. As Jesus, the great storyteller, said, "The truth will set you free" (John 8:32). The truth can set us free from the prison of negative, unhelpful stories. In freedom, we can devise new stories, ones that offer us the possibilities of a new marriage with a new future.

Try this:

1. Think of an emotional interaction that happened between you and your spouse today. Write it down as a story. Now, revisit your narrative. Does it include right brain information, such as bodily sensations, memories, and emotions? If any of these elements are missing from the account, add them into your story, even if you have to make educated guesses.

2. Now, rewrite your story from the perspective of your spouse. Notice how different it feels to write the narrative from someone else's point of view. How do you think your spouse feels? What memories were evoked for him or her? How does writing the story from your spouse's vantage point feel different from your own perspective?

3. Revisit the narrative for a third time. Slowly, consider the following questions. In my story, do I accept any responsibility for the difficulty between us? Does my account explicitly uncover a significant fear that I felt in that situation? Is it possible that my narrative contains some fiction? Does this account portray my spouse in a positive or negative light? Pay attention to the feelings that arise as you consider these questions.

4. Sit in quiet prayer for a few minutes, and then rewrite the story. Don't think of it as your story. Cast aside any efforts to protect yourself or make yourself look good. Instead, concentrate on authoring a story that will be helpful as you attempt to learn from the incident and move forward. Try to compose a version of the event that would satisfy both you and your spouse. What emotions does this exercise evoke?

CHAPTER 7

Behavior

*I don't know what I'm doing, because I don't do what
I want to do. Instead, I do the thing that I hate.*
—Romans 7:15

Picture yourself placing dominoes in a long line, one after another.
The challenge is to place the tiles properly so that when you tip the
first tile, eventually the last one falls. As a young boy, I played dominoes over and over. Now, as an adult, I see my body, mind, and behavior working according to this same "domino effect."

I want you to imagine six tiles lined up in a row. One of the end
pieces stands for your body, while the other one symbolizes your
behavior. In the middle are four bones representing the activities of
your mind. If one tile moves, they are all affected. How do we come to
understand how the tile labeled "behavior" is influenced by and influences the other five pieces? To answer this question, we will examine
two myths that affect our understanding of behavior, an essential part
of relationships.

Myth #1: Behavior is the place to start.

To Rachel, a massage therapist, and David, the owner of a landscape design business, behavior was the obvious place to begin

working on their marriage. At times, they treated each other well, and when they did, they felt close and satisfied with their relationship. However, at other times they found themselves succumbing to negative actions. When David was tired, he would be extremely critical of and mean to Rachel. She then found herself withdrawing in response. In this state, she became insensitive to and uncaring about his needs. "If only we could change our behavior, everything would be okay," they complained.

According to some self-help authors, behavior is the first step in modifying our marital relationship. They suggest that good behavior will bring about positive feelings and better thinking. However, according to both recent findings in neuroscience and the Christian contemplative tradition, this idea is confusing and misleading.

Referring back to the row of dominoes, where should our effort to change begin? Scientific and Christian contemplative thought are converging on a shared belief about where behavior stands in the row of tiles: last. First, an episode in our marriage triggers a physical reaction. Once our body gets out of balance, a chain reaction of mental events begins to happen: painful memories, powerful emotions, and unhelpful stories emerge. Once these extreme alterations happen to our body and mind, negative behaviors are sure to follow. Before we realize it, we have moved from love to war, and we are engaged in behaviors that sabotage our personal and relational well-being.

In order to better understand a destructive action, we need to know what causes it. What starts this chain reaction that eventually leads to bad behavior? In looking for an explanation, we tend to see our spouses—and them alone—as the source of their behavior.[110] Perhaps they have some bad trait, or a psychological problem, or some other inadequacy that causes their awful behavior. However, the author of the book of Romans did not view the person as the source of misdirected actions. Instead, he claimed that the cause was sin (Romans 7:17, 20). Now, what is sin? According to the Christian contemplative tradition, *sin* is the sense of being cut off from God, other people, and the true self.[111] This is the real basis of our bad behavior.

On this subject—that is, the origins of destructive actions— scientific and Christian contemplative thinkers are in agreement. They concur that separation and the sense of insecurity it produces triggers our threat response system. It is this self-protection system that tips over the first tile: a physical reaction. Then, the chain reaction of mental events is set in motion until the last bone—behavior—topples. The system for protecting ourselves gets turned on with the tipping of the first tile, and eventually shows up as behavior that hurts the person we love the most.

Returning to Rachel and David, what triggered their threat response systems? For Rachel, David's "mean" behavior alerted her safety system. Once she perceived that he was being "abusive," a signal went off in her head that said, "You don't have to take this!" For David, an alarm of separation and insecurity sounded when Rachel withdrew. He desired her responsiveness, but receiving only indifference, he felt vulnerable and afraid.

The temptation to focus on behavior is understandable because a person's actions are so obvious. We can't help but see a look of contempt, or hear a loud voice and words of criticism, or feel the chill of a cold shoulder. Our mind quickly decides: "Behavior is the real problem." However, modern scientists and Christian contemplatives agree that the targeting of behavior is misleading.

I believe that an overemphasis on behavior can distract us from more critical issues. Let me illustrate with a personal story. It was the summer after sixth grade, and I was playing my favorite game: baseball. On this particular night, I kept swinging at and missing all the balls. After the game, the coach—my dad—asked me what was wrong. I told him that I had trouble seeing the ball. Soon after, I was evaluated by the optometrist and learned that I had developed a vision problem. Returning to my next game with glasses, and improved vision, I found that my hitting returned to normal.

This story illustrates the importance of focusing on the right thing. My dad could have zeroed in on my bad behavior—my substandard hitting. However, instead of concentrating on my batting, he targeted the crucial issue—my poor eyesight. Once the real difficulty was solved, the behavior improved.

In the case of Rachel and David, they were concentrating on the other person's behavior. To Rachel, it was obvious that David failed to complement her on her attempts to make his life easier. Instead, he found some small thing to criticize. And David couldn't miss the fact that when Rachel withdrew to another room for the evening and he asked her a question she declined to respond.

If behavior is not the real problem, then where do we start? According to modern scientific thinking and ancient contemplative thought, our mind is the place to begin. This belief appears early in the Christian contemplative tradition with the Desert Fathers and Mothers—often referred to as the "Christian psychologists of the church."[112] Until recently, their ideas from the third and fourth centuries were sealed away in a set of Latin volumes called the *Patrologia Latina,* but Thomas Merton made the desert teachings available for the first time in a contemporary, accessible way in a book called *The Wisdom of the Desert.*[113] Setting the trajectory for Christian contemplative thought, these Desert Fathers and Mothers placed little emphasis on something clear to all: behavior. Instead, they concentrated on something that was mysterious, dark, and not clearly visible. They aspired for things like the true self, love, and purity of heart. In the modern language of neuroscience and psychology, these ambitions would be referred to as aspects of the mind.

The real trouble is rooted in our mind. As long as the mind is out of balance and under the control of the threat response system, it will move us toward behavior that threatens our marriage. Once the mind gets out of balance and its mental properties—self, memories, emotions, narratives—begin to fall, inevitably behavior will topple.

Therefore, our goal must be to calm and soothe the mind.[114] Part II of this book will focus on this objective. Focusing our attention on the right thing—training the mind through contemplation—will enable us to return to loving behaviors.

Myth #2: We can separate the behavior of spouses.

Most of us believe that our behavior is distinct from our spouse's. We think: "I am over here, and you are over there. There is a gulf that separates us." However, findings from neuroscience confirm an old contemplative concept that we are interconnected, or one. Daniel Siegel makes a related claim: "The mind is a relational process. Energy and information flow between and among people."[115] Let's examine this assertion. First, Siegel is arguing that the mind is something that is shared—or that flows—between persons. Second, since behavior falls in the same direction as the mind, then we can argue that behavior also flows between individuals. Scientific research shows that, without words, we are picking up on not only the sensations, feelings, and thoughts of our spouse, but also their behavior.

Building on this idea that minds and behavior are connected, it makes sense to think of behavior as having a circular flow. This concept of circularity is revolutionary because we are generally taught a linear view of behavior. For example: "My spouse's behavior caused my behavior"; A caused B. This view enables us to point an accusing finger at our spouse, blame him or her for causing our marital problems, and thus let ourselves off the hook: "I am only acting this way because you made me."

Rachel and David had employed a linear view of behavior. She claimed that her withdrawal was caused by his meanness. As a result, she took the moral high ground, claiming that she was nice until he started acting badly. On the other hand, David perceived that his anger was a reasonable response to her bitter withdrawal. "Wouldn't you get mad if your wife ignored you?" he asked. To him, it was clear that she was to blame.

Linear thinking leads us to blame the one who "started it," but there is another competing explanation for behavior: a circular view. According to circular thinking, behavior looks this way: A causes B and B causes A. According to this theory, the negative interaction between spouses has no starting point. Rather, their behavior is mutually caused. How we act prior to our spouse's behavior and how we respond to their actions are now part of the overall picture. Now, we cannot exclude ourselves from responsibility. Most marital therapists agree that the deterioration of marital relationships, rather than being caused by the behavior of one spouse, is the result of negative interactional cycles.[116]

There are two different ways of understanding the interactional patterns in which couples find themselves. Andrew Christensen and Neil Jacobson, co-creators of Integrative Behavioral Couple Therapy (IBCT), offer the first model. They propose that an interpersonal problem includes both a provocative behavior and a vulnerability.[117] The provocative behavior refers to our partner doing something that has the potential to hurt us. The vulnerability is explained by something in our history, something that makes us especially reactive to threats of abandonment, the absence of recognition, or the lack of control. I like the analogy provided by Christensen and Jacobson. They say the provocation is like a bee sting that causes an allergic reaction because of that person's vulnerabilities—or "psychological allergies."[118] Who do we condemn for the difficulty? Rather than blame one partner, the focus should be on the responsibility they share.

When we apply this model of understanding to Rachel and David, we can see how they each engaged in a provocative behavior and they each displayed a vulnerability. David's criticism of Rachel revealed her vulnerability to unkind words. (During her childhood, she could never please her parents.) And Rachel's withdrawal showed how sensitive David was to her neglect. (When he was a child, David's dad was preoccupied with family problems, so his dad seldom had time to focus on him.)

A second model for understanding interpersonal problems focuses on extremes in arousal.[119] When exposed to threats, the bodies and minds of some people lean toward hyper-arousal, which prepares them to attack their partner. For others, when their threat response system is activated, their bodies and minds shut down—which we refer to as hypo-arousal or under-arousal—and they simply withdraw. Based upon this model of extremes, we can determine two opposite forms of behavior: attack and withdraw.

Returning to the concept of interactional patterns, we can now identify three common cycles: withdraw-withdraw, attack-attack, and attack-withdraw.[120] The first two arrangements are most familiar. The withdraw-withdraw sequence, regular in low-arousal couples, is characterized by fear that isolates their lives and cools their marriage. On the other hand, the attack-attack cycle, common in high-arousal couples, is characterized by anger that quickly accelerates like a fire.

Applying this second model to Rachel and David, we can easily recognize their pattern: the anger-withdrawal cycle. When Rachel perceived—by his criticism—that David was angry, she withdrew. Upon seeing that Rachel had distanced herself, David became irritated and infuriated. And then, his outrage prompted Rachel to draw back even more. You can see how they became trapped in this vicious, ongoing pattern of behavior.

Susan Johnson, the creator of Emotionally Focused Couple Therapy, suggests a unique approach for dealing with these negative interactional patterns.[121] Her technique, called *externalizing*, describes the destructive cycle—not people—as the problem. By adopting this mentality, we can frame the interactional sequence as the enemy, as opposed to defining our partner as the adversary. Using Johnson's approach, the pattern is now viewed as having taken over the relationship. Therefore, the couple must unite in their efforts to free themselves from the destructive cycle that is robbing them of the security and marital satisfaction that they both desire. Working as a team, they can now combine their efforts to put out the fire that threatens to destroy their marriage.

In order to put out a blaze, we must understand something about the nature of a fire. The first phase, called the incipient stage, is usually represented as a very small flame. Very quickly, the fire can enter its second and third stages, which are extremely dangerous. The final phase, called the decay stage, refers to the time when the blaze starts to die down because it is receiving less fuel. Nevertheless, this last stage is still volatile because the introduction of new oxygen or material can ignite a new fire, called a backdraft. Fire experts agree that the best time to intervene is during the first stage of a blaze. This is the best time to put out the flame and prevent its destruction.

When it comes to the fires that quickly ignite in our marriages, it is best to respond quickly. The first step in putting out a relational blaze is to recognize it. The first sign of a flame is that unpleasant smell of insecurity. As the fire heats up, our body moves out of its normal range of arousal. Then, we take a position of either attack or withdrawal. Hopefully, one or both partners will say, "The cycle is trying to get started. It is looking for fuel." Now, with the fire in its earliest stage, you have the best opportunity for putting out a flame that has the potential to burn down your marriage.

Hopefully, in this chapter you have gained a better understanding of destructive behavior. First, we learned that behavior is the last occurrence in a series of mental events that are set in motion by a system that is designed to protect us. In addition, we observed that this series of events—which eventually culminates in behavior—is triggered by feelings of separation, disconnection, and insecurity. Finally, we examined the notion that behavior is interconnected.

This understanding leads us to some basic strategies for preventing and responding to destructive behaviors. First, we must pay attention to our state of mind. When we notice that our mind has moved out of a calm and relaxed state, that our threat response system has been activated, we can work toward calming and soothing our mind. This early intervention can prevent eventual bad behavior. Second, it is vital that we protect the sense of security that we experience in our marriage. Without this sense of connection, we cannot maintain the mental balance that promotes pro-relationship behavior. Next, it is important to avoid blaming our spouse for the behavior that is causing any marital problems. Instead, we need to assume mutual responsibility for causing and stopping the negative interactional patterns that are interfering with our intimate relationship. By working together to fight a behavioral cycle, we can stop a fire in its earliest stage so we can protect our marriage, which is of inestimable worth.

Try this:

1. Reflect upon some undesirable way that you interacted with your spouse today. First, identify and put words to it. For example, "I acted distant and uninterested in my spouse." Ask yourself what triggered this behavior. Did your spouse do something unpleasant that preceded your reaction? (Since we can identify an action by our spouse that precedes our reaction, we often assume that our spouse "caused" us to act a certain way.) Now, entertain the idea

that your behavior may have been triggered by a sense of separation, disconnection, or insecurity. Is this a possibility?

2. Reflect upon another unpleasant interaction between you and your spouse. First, describe it in terms of actions. That is, "She did this and I did that." Now, shift your attention to your body and mind. How did your body respond in that situation? With less or more energy? What was your emotional reaction? Did you feel angry, hurt, afraid? Did the event bring up any past memories? What did you notice yourself saying about your spouse, your marriage, or yourself? What happened when you switched your attention from your behavior to your body and mind?

3. Select an event between yourself and your spouse that did not go well. First, map it out in a linear fashion. That is, A caused B. Second, use a circular design. That is, A caused B and B caused A. Did you do something that hurt your spouse? What do you think your spouse's vulnerability was? Did your spouse do something that hurt your feelings? What was it from your past that made you vulnerable? Finally, identify your interactional cycle. Did your spouse withdraw or attack? Did you withdraw or attack?

4. Using the last part of the previous exercise, consider externalizing the interactional cycle. Put it into words. That is, describe the pattern as something that is trying to destroy your marriage. Identify how it is damaging your relationship. Finally, describe how you and your spouse are going to join forces to defeat this destructive enemy.

PART II

Renewing Your Mind

CHAPTER 8

Contemplative Prayer

Sooner or later each one of us must succumb to our contemplative longing and gain either the courage or recklessness to begin our contemplative journey.
—*John O'Donohue, Beauty*

So far, we have established one major point: the mind is the basic cause of our marital problems. When the mind gets out of balance, it begins to sabotage not only our personal well-being, but also the health of our most intimate relationship. The necessary response is obvious. We need to restore stability to the mind. But how do we accomplish this task? In the last three decades, science has begun to echo an old Christian answer to this question: through contemplative practice. Daniel Siegel points toward a growing body of research that demonstrates that contemplative practices can strengthen minds and marriages.[122]

In this part of the book we will turn to Christian contemplative prayer. While other religious forms have important things to say about contemplative methods, this book will stay within the Christian tradition. My goal in this second section is to focus on how Centering Prayer is practiced and understood within the context of the Christian contemplative path. We will learn how contemplative prayer can change our mind, and by renewing our mind, we will discover how to transform our marriage.

Where does this process of renewal begin? It begins with the understanding that our mind easily loses it balance. The Irish poet William Butler Yeats captures this characteristic of the mind in his poem, "The Balloon of the Mind":[123]

> *Hands, do what you're bid;*
> *Bring the balloon of the mind*
> *That bellies and drags in the wind*
> *Into its narrow shed.*

In this poem, Yeats compares the mind to the hot air balloons that were popular in his day. You may know that the lift of a hot air balloon is largely dependent on the temperature of the air, something the pilot cannot control. Carried on the wind, the ride of the balloon can be rough, unpredictable, and even disastrous. (The world's first aviation disaster was the crash of a hot air balloon in Ireland in 1785.)

Our mind can operate much like a hot air balloon. Mental functions can quickly succumb to unconscious influences and mental processes, and as a result, we quit steering our mind. Once the mind gets caught in the strong winds of physical sensations, memories, emotions, and narratives, we become like helpless passengers in the basket, at the mercy of the strong currents of air. Lifted on the turbulent winds of chaos, the mind can wreak havoc and destroy our lives.

Ron, whom we met along with his wife, Natalie, in chapter 3, was surprised to discover how active his mind was when he sat down for Centering Prayer. He reported: "I begin with the intent of focusing my attention on God but my mind won't cooperate. Before I realize it, I am thinking about a check that I need to write for my daughter's piano teacher. Or I find myself replaying a difficult conversation that I had the day before with my wife. Or my mind starts rehearsing a talk that I have to give at work. Or I start paying attention to my tooth that has started hurting. I wonder what may be wrong with it and think that I need to make an appointment with my dentist. My mind seems to have an endless supply of things to think about."

What are we to do? Yeats offers us a solution—that is, to "bring the balloon of the mind . . . into its narrow shed." When brought inside, out of the strong breezes, the balloon of the mind begins to perform quite differently. It no longer thrashes about in the wind. Instead, it becomes quiet and silent in the shelter. If we apply contemplative language to this metaphor, we could say that the narrow shed is contemplative prayer. Contemplative prayer can restore balance and bring calmness to the mind. And in this structure of prayer, the mind is now free to travel into another dimension, a spiritual one.

John O'Donohue, another Irish poet, in describing the relationship between the mind and contemplative prayer, introduces another metaphor. He says that the mind is like a tower of windows.[124] Sadly, many people remain trapped, looking out of only one opening. In other words, they repeatedly keep watching the world, themselves, and their marriage through the same mind. They keep viewing their marital relationship through the same memories, emotions, and narratives day after day. However, growth and change come about when we draw back from that window, turn, and walk around to another opening through which we can view the events of our life. Fortunately, "the mind always has at least one window facing the eternal."[125] The window that we are interested in is the frame of contemplative prayer.

Centuries before O'Donohue described contemplative prayer with his metaphor of a window facing the eternal, Jesus said that prayer was like entering a room. According to Thomas Keating, the primary architect of Centering Prayer, contemplative prayer is patterned after this formula.[126] The first step in this blueprint is to move into a secret place, a place inside. Henri Nouwen, the Harvard professor and Christian contemplative, writes, "Once we come to know that inner, holy place, a place more beautiful and precious than any place we can travel to, we want to be there and be spiritually fed."[127]

I wonder: "What is this inner room like?" The Christian spiritual

tradition has two basic answers to this question.[128] The first perspective
is that this inner room is bathed in light. In other words, it is visible,
describable, and open to thinking. In this space, a person can use pic-
tures, words, and intellect to communicate with God in prayer. This
view, called the kataphatic path, has given birth to meditative prayer, a
process of quiet reflection and thinking about some topic. In meditation, practitioners concentrate their attention on some object, such as a
picture, sound, phrase, or word. Meditation is something that we seem
to be able to do and accomplish on our own.

The second perspective describes this inner room as void of light—
or dark. This second way—called apophatic—emphasizes that God lies
behind, beyond, and hidden from the intellect. The apophatic approach
has given birth to contemplative prayer, which involves refraining from
thinking. Instead of thinking, practitioners quiet their mental activities
in order to be silent and passive before God. What comes as a result is
considered a gift.

As people enter into Christian contemplative prayer, they typically
find themselves practicing one of these two types of contemplation:
awareness or surrender.[129] For both methods, the goal is the same—that
is, to quiet the mind and to enter into a silent space, void of light. With
the awareness method, one simply watches mental processes—bodily
sensations, memories, emotions, narratives, impulses to act—rise, take
form, and dissipate. On the other hand, with surrender methods, as
soon as a thought emerges into consciousness, one simply lets it go.
The approach that I teach couples, called Centering Prayer, falls into
this second category: surrender.

Within the Christian apophatic tradition, the metaphor of darkness
is often used to help us understand this process of letting go of mental
processes. The word "dark," instead of implying that something bad or
evil is happening, has a very different meaning. It simply suggests that
the normal mind cannot comprehend or understand what is happening when mental functions cease.[130] When John of the Cross—from
sixteenth century Spain—employs the image of darkness, he is trying

to teach us that something outside of our awareness happens when we engage in contemplative prayer.[131] He writes, "Contemplation is secret wisdom, hidden from the workings of intellect and other faculties."[132] This idea that prayer can happen at a level that is unseen by the conscious mind is clearly captured by the Apostle Paul when he wrote, "We don't know what we should pray, but the Spirit itself pleads our case with unexpressed groans" (Romans 8:26).

To contemplatives, this idea that prayer happens at a level concealed from the intelligent mind speaks to the mysterious nature of contemplative prayer. In contemplative prayer, we embrace an experience that our normal thinking is unable to understand. We surrender to a process that our ordinary intellect cannot explain. We can befriend what happens at this level of the mind, but we cannot comprehend it. The experience is beyond all words and comprehension.

According to John of the Cross, when we enter into this darkness, we find ourselves recovering our love of mystery.[133] Do you remember your love of mystery as a child? You imagined all kinds of possibilities. You created worlds in which anything was possible. There were no limitations. That is what the contemplative life is, a slow process of becoming like little children (Matthew 18:3). When we become like a child, we fall in love with mystery again.

Entering into the mystery of contemplative prayer is like entering a land of darkness. Our ordinary mind cannot see what is happening in secret. Mystery can be experienced, sensed, felt, appreciated, and even loved, but it cannot be understood. All we can do is open ourselves to it. As Gerald May writes, "We do not embrace it in our arms, it embraces us. We do not capture it but are captured by it."[134] Entering into the darkness of mystery may seem scary, but it is also beautiful. As Albert Einstein once said, "The most beautiful experience we can have is the mysterious."[135]

Mystery is beautiful because it does something to the normal functions of our mind. It creates space in our mind for awe, reverence, and wonder. John O'Donohue notes, "Wonder is the child of mystery."[136]

This sense of wonder allows our mind to explore new possibilities, bringing freshness and originality to our thinking. When we feel wonder, we regain a sense of reverence before God. As we surrender to the mysterious process that happens during contemplative prayer, God is able to transform and balance our mind.

So what do we do with our normal mental functions during contemplative prayer? According to Thomas Merton, the ordinary mind has no real job to do during contemplative prayer.[137] During this time of prayer, we let go of the mind's usual activities—sensing, feeling, remembering, planning, narrating, etc.—and the noise of the mind falls into the background. We resist the urge to engage in the normal capacities of reason, memory, and emotion. Contemplative prayer is about breaking up "the tyranny of the mind."[138]

My patient Ron was pleased to report that his mind would sometimes get quiet during his times of Centering Prayer. He described the times of mental silence this way: "I seem to lose track of place. . . . I forget about the chair and room that I am in. I also can forget about time. It's only when I start thinking again that I become aware that time has passed. I think I could describe the time of quiet as emptiness . . . but in a good way. Even though the time is usually brief, I feel a deep sense of peace."

One amazing thing that happens during contemplative prayer, when the normal functions of the mind cease, is that the contents of the unconscious mind appear. According to Thomas Merton, as the mind becomes quiet, "the doors of your subconscious mind fall ajar and all sorts of curious figures begin to come waltzing about on the scene."[139] Here, I think Merton is pointing to the emergence of forgotten memories of ourselves and significant people: grandparents, parents, siblings, etc. Following in the footsteps of Merton, Thomas Keating agrees that Centering Prayer releases the energies of the unconscious.[140] This means that physical sensations, memories, and emotions from the past can emerge and be healed during times of quiet, contemplative prayer. The damage that accumulates in our body and nervous system over a lifetime can be evacuated and healed as the body and mind enter into the deep rest of contemplative prayer.

In one session, Ron connected the discussion with his practice of Centering Prayer: "I have been surprised by some strong physical sensations during my times of Centering Prayer. Sometimes, I get so hot that I start perspiring, and I may even start feeling nauseous. The sensations were stronger when I first started, but they are less frequent now. I think these strong physical reactions are related to my history of being disconnected from my body and emotions."

Ron went on to describe a recent memory and emotion that had arisen abruptly during his time of prayer: "As I so often do during my time of Centering Prayer, I was being hard on myself, thinking that I wasn't doing it right. Then I noticed this strong feeling of guilt. Where is that coming from, I wondered. Out of the blue, I remembered my father saying, 'Ron, that's not good enough.' I was lost in a memory from my elementary school years. I had been working on a project with my dad and had done my best, but I remember him saying, 'You didn't do it right.' There was that same old guilt. It seems that guilt is my favorite miserable feeling."

In addition to a release of unconscious material, there is a second thing that happens in the absence of mental activity during contemplative prayer: our mind moves from its normal way of thinking to the midpoint of our being.[141] This idea speaks to different levels of awareness. At the outer or surface plane, the mind works in its normal fashion. However, at the center, we cannot comprehend the workings of the mind. Merton writes, "At the center of our being is a point which is inaccessible to the fantasies of our own mind."[142] At the core level of awareness, our own nature as a person and the Divine become more and more interwoven.

If the normal mind has no real job during Centering Prayer, then what are we supposed to be doing during this time? Our main task is to simply focus our intention on being with God. Our main goal is not, as some people think, to work hard to eliminate thoughts or words. This may sometimes happen as a result of focusing our attention on God, but the primary goal is to simply spend time with God. Being open is essentially about being receptive. We cannot make anything spiritual happen on our own, but day by day, we can set aside time to sit with a stance of receptive openness to God.[143]

Once we have done our job, the rest is up to Him. This concept reminds me of sailing. I live in the mountains of North Carolina, but I always enjoy visiting the coast and watching people sail. I understand that the skills of sailing are primarily about how sails are placed in the air and how the hull of the boat is situated in the water. There are five basic sailing skills: tracking and jibing, reducing sail, sail trimming, hull trimming, and heeling. These are things the sailor can do. However, the sailor cannot do anything to control wind and water speeds. These are the forces of nature that provide the energy to move the boat forward. They are gifts. Once sailor has done his job, the rest is up to nature.

We can learn and practice certain skills related to contemplative prayer, but God does the rest. What God does is considered a gift. We can neither predict, control, or even understand the actions of God that take place during contemplative prayer. We are much like the sailor, who, after training and learning the necessary skills, simply has to wait on the wind. Jesus captured this idea when he said, "God's Spirit blows wherever it wishes. You hear its sound, but you don't know where it comes from or where it is going" (John 3:8). When the wind shows up, it is simply a gift.

One of the reasons I recommend Centering Prayer to couples is because it teaches the practitioner specific skills. These abilities are captured in four straightforward guidelines:[144]

1. Choose a sacred word as the symbol of your intention to consent to God's presence and action within (for example: love, peace, Jesus, etc.).
2. Sit comfortably with your eyes closed, and silently introduce the sacred word as the symbol of your consent to God's presence and action within.

3. When engaged with your thoughts, return ever-so-gently to the sacred word.
4. At the end of the prayer period, remain in silence with your eyes closed for a couple minutes.

At this point, it may be useful to recall the illustration of the sailor. Like the sailor, as we employ the four guidelines of Centering Prayer, we are learning important skills. These skills have the power to transform our minds. In the rest of part II, we will focus on four basic skills: stillness, attention, openness, and letting go. We will then examine how these abilities become translated into two essential qualities: union and love.

We have learned that the ordinary mind is prone to extremes: chaos versus rigidity, over-arousal versus under-arousal, and fight versus flight. However, contemplative prayer offers us a path in the middle. This course has the power to bring stability to our mind and health to our marriage. Let's now turn our attention to the first skill of contemplative prayer: stillness.

Try this:

1. Are you attracted to a method of prayer that involves refraining from thinking, one that relies on letting go of the mind's usual activities?

2. Are you open to a type of prayer that happens at a level that is unseen by the conscious mind? In other words, do you want to examine a form of prayer in which the ordinary mind cannot understand what is happening?

3. What do you think about the primary goal of contemplative prayer: spending time with God?

CHAPTER 9

Stillness

Be still, and know that I am God.
—*Psalm 46:10*

*The tools of the contemplative are the finesse
and rigour of stillness and silence.*
—*John O'Donohue, Beauty*

At the heart of Centering Prayer is silence.[145] Quietness and seren- ity can bring balance to the mind, but the mind resists this state of calm. Instead, the mind seems drawn to restless activity and incessant noise. So how can we quiet the mind? Our first inclination is to bring serenity to the mind by working with it directly, making deliberate efforts to restrain it from its wandering ways. However, before turning our attention in this direction, let's consider another option. Centering Prayer points us first to the body. Let me remind you of a short phrase in the second guideline of Centering Prayer: "sitting comfortably."[146]

Bringing silence and stability to the mind begins by introducing stillness to the body. We must recognize the place of the body in the contemplative journey. In contemplative prayer, we cannot be like Mr. Duffy, a character created by James Joyce, who "lived a little distant from his body."[147] Instead of feeling alienated from our body, we must learn to locate ourselves in it. As David Benner, the Christian psychologist and contemplative, says, "Feeling at home anywhere starts with feeling at home in our bodies."[148]

You may be wondering, "Why do we need to start with our body?" From a scientific perspective, Antonio Damasio claims that we have to start with the body because it is the foundation of the mind.[149] When the mind's threat system is activated, the body moves out of its desired, narrow range of functioning. When the body gets out of balance, the mind is sure to follow. Therefore, neuroscience teaches us that calming the mind starts by calming the body.

During my childhood, one of my favorite games to play in the pool was a game we called "chicken." Each team had two people, one member sitting on the shoulders of his teammate. The object of the game was to knock the opposing team over by getting the person on the bottom to lose his balance. I remember being on top at times. If the person on bottom lost his balance and fell over, there was nothing I could do. I was helpless and sure to fall as well. This is the way it is with the body and mind. The mind rests on the body.

James Finley, a Christian psychologist and contemplative, offers a common sense answer to why we need to start with the body: because we always know where it is.[150] That may sound odd, but think about it. Do you always know where your mind is? Perhaps you are talking to your spouse but your mind is somewhere else. Instead of following what your spouse is saying, you are preoccupied with an event from earlier in the day, or fearful of a meeting that is scheduled for tomorrow. And what about that common experience of arriving at a destination in your car and thinking, "I haven't noticed a thing. What have I been thinking about?" We may not always be able to locate our mind, but we will always know where our body is.

How do we go about stilling the body so that the mind becomes silent? The Centering Prayer answer is simple: sit. Sitting is more important than we imagine. Blaise Pascal, the seventeenth-century French mathematician and Christian contemplative, claimed: "All human evil comes from a single cause, man's inability to sit still in a room." Sitting still in prayer has a powerful impact on the mind. In C. S. Lewis's *The Screwtape Letters*, Wormwood, the young demon-in-training, is instructed by his uncle, Screwtape, regarding the role of the body in prayer. "My Dear Wormwood, . . . they constantly forget, what you must always remember, that they are animals and that whatever their bodies do affects their souls."[151]

The body makes two important contributions to contemplative prayer. The first is physical stillness. Basil Pennington, a co-developer of Centering Prayer, instructs practitioners to sit still for twenty minutes.[152] In keeping with the idea that what we do with our body affects our mind, Christian contemplatives have come to see the benefits of an erect and stable sitting posture. Pennington says that one should be both comfortable and that one's back should be straight when practicing Centering Prayer. Posture is an important part of prayer. Since many people don't know what to do with their hands, I recommend that they just lay them, palms down, on their knees or cup them in their lap.[153]

Sitting still may sound rather easy, but Barbara, who you met in chapter 2 along with her husband Mike, found it to be just the opposite. She described her experience this way: "Typically, I feel a bit restless and sometimes fidgety. At times, I have the physical sensation of feeling itchy. First, one place will itch and then another. It is very distracting and unpleasant. Sometimes, I will start feeling very uncomfortable. First, one part and then another part of my body will start aching or hurting. I just can't seem to get comfortable."

The second important contribution of the body during contemplative prayer is breathing. From early on, Christians have associated breath with spirit. An ancient word for spirit is the Hebrew word *ruah*, which is also the word for air or wind.[154] We read in Scripture that God breathed on the first man and he received life (Genesis 2:7). After his resurrection, we read that Jesus met with his disciples, breathed on them, and gave them the Spirit (John 20:22). In contemplative prayer, we open our sails to receive the wind (or breath) of the Spirit.

Because of its close proximity, breath becomes a powerful contem-

plative metaphor for the closeness of God. As we pay attention to our
breathing during contemplative prayer, we are reminded that God—
like our breathing—is not far from us. Using our breath to remind us
of God's presence reminds us that we do not have to restlessly search
the world for God, because He is as nearby as our breath. Christian
contemplative Martin Laird quotes Saint Augustine as saying, "Why do
we rush about . . . looking for God who is here at home with us, if all we
want to do is be with him?"[155]

As early as the fourth century, there has been an awareness of the
role of breath in contemplative prayer.[156] One of the earliest examples
comes from an instruction that the famous Christian monk, Macarius,
gave to Evagrius. Martin Laird quotes Marcarius as telling Evagrius to
say with each breath, "Our Lord Jesus, have mercy on me: I bless thee,
my Lord Jesus, help me."[157] John Climacus, a seventh-century monk on
Mount Sinai, is known for saying, "Let the remembrance of Jesus be
with your every breath."[158]

This tradition of uniting the Jesus prayer with breathing continued
to be preserved and cultivated by the Orthodox tradition.[159] In the
fourteenth century, at least two important figures advocated practicing
the Jesus prayer with breath. In his work *Those Who Practice the Life
of Stillness,* Saint Gregory Palamas is quoted as saying, "Some teachers recommend them [beginners] to pay attention to the exhalation
and inhalation of their breath."[160] Nicephorous the Solitary, a monk of
Mount Athos in Greece, addressing the connection between prayer,
breathing, and the mind, is quoted as saying, "Having collected your
mind with you, lead it into the channel of breathing."[161]

This tradition of using the breath as an aid in contemplation, which
was developed in the context of the Jesus prayer tradition, appears
in Centering Prayer. Even though the four guidelines for Centering
Prayer do not contain any direct references to breathing, the breath is
addressed in other discussions about Centering Prayer. For example,
Thomas Keating says that noticing or being aware of our breathing can
be an expression of our intention to consent to God's presence and

action within us.[162] Basil Pennington offers a simple breathing exercise that helps relieve practitioners of bodily tension as they prepare
for Centering Prayer.[163] He recommends inhaling and exhaling deeply
three times. This time of relaxation prepares the practitioner for step
one of Centering Prayer.

Barbara, like others I work with, finds that focusing on her breath
during Centering Prayer often helps her still her body and mind. She
put it this way: "I sometimes use my breath as my sacred word. When
my mind wanders, I simply let go of the immediate thought by focusing
on my breathing. The physical sensations of breathing, such as hearing
the sound or noticing the falling of my chest, are comforting and help
calm me down."

A beautiful poem by the Irish poet R. S. Thomas called "The Moor"
captures where our conversation has been and where it will lead:[164]

It was like a church to me.
I entered it on soft foot,
Breath held like a cap in the hand.
It was quiet.
What God was there made himself felt,
Not listened to, in clean colours
That brought a moistening of the eye,
In movement of the wind over grass.

There were no prayers said. But stillness
Of the heart's passions—that was praise
Enough; and the mind's cession
Of its kingdom. I walked on,
Simple and poor, while the air crumbled
And broke on me generously as bread.

In this poem, Thomas creates an image of prayer that includes
breath. The prayer is quiet, missing the chatter of the intellect. In spite

of the absence of words, there is the presence of stillness. And what happens when he enters into stillness? The mind gives up the rights to its kingdom. Through the stillness of the body, the mind becomes silent. It relinquishes control, stops looking for privilege and power, abstains from demands for justice and fairness, and gives up reason. In short, it relinquishes its kingdom. For a period of time, the normal mind ceases from its normal activities.

There was a time during my elementary years that I was in love with bicycles. My friends and I were like a pack of animals on wheels. For a short period of time, we hit upon the idea of attaching small pieces of paper to the spokes. When we rode, the paper, flapping against the frame, caused a din of noise. I loved it all—the sound and the speed. There was one boy in the neighborhood who we all feared: Danny. He scared us because, if given the opportunity, he would poke a stick between the spokes as we rode. If he succeeded, the bike would come to sudden halt.

My mind often reminds me of those noisy bicycles from childhood. But contemplative prayer offers us the opportunity to bring stillness and silence to our restless mind. Cynthia Bourgeault says that contemplative prayer is "essentially about putting a stick into the spokes of our normal whirling wheel of thinking in order to break up the tyranny of the mind."[165] The stillness of contemplative prayer can usher in silence of the mind. In silence, the normal mind gives up its control. During this period of freedom from the mind's tyranny, we are ushered into another kingdom. This is not the kingdom of mind with which we are familiar; this is the kingdom of God.

Now—in stillness and silence—we have arrived at the ultimate goal of contemplative prayer. John O'Donohue writes, "In stillness, the silence of the Divine becomes intimate."[166] When the mind becomes silent, we are able to hear the voice of God. Christian contemplatives often make a paradoxical claim—that is, "Silence is God's first language."[167] And as we listen closely, we hear the language of love.

Under the tyranny of the normal mind, we see a veil between God and ourselves. God seems so distant. However, as the mind becomes silent, we enter the spiritual level of our being. In this place, during contemplative prayer, we recognize the closeness and presence of God. We realize that we are not separate, as the normal mind would convince us. God becomes as close as our breath, and we hear the calming sound of that breath as we inhale and exhale. And the words heard in the wind are, "I love you. Welcome home."

Try this:

1. Take some time to discover what helps you sit comfortably. How does the height of the chair affect your comfort level? (For example, some people report that sitting with their hips a little higher than their knees is more comfortable.) Work with your posture some. Does putting a pillow behind your back help? Notice the position of your hands. Which position is more relaxing?

2. Before you begin your time of Centering Prayer, take a moment to be aware of your body. Say to yourself, "Right now, I am sitting in this chair, in this room. I can feel my feet on the floor and my body resting in this chair."

3. Experiment with Basil Pennington's exercise as you prepare for Centering Prayer. Inhale and exhale deeply three times before you begin step one.

4. Experiment with using your breath as your sacred word. When your mind wanders, focus on your breathing as a reminder of your intention to consent to the presence and action of God.

CHAPTER 10

Attention

I don't know exactly what prayer is.
I do know how to pay attention, how to fall down
into the grass, how to kneel down in the grass,
how to be idle and blessed, how to stroll through the fields,
which is what I have been doing all day.
Tell me, what else should I have done?
Doesn't everything die at last, and too soon?
Tell me, what is it you plan to do
With your one wild and precious life?
        —Mary Oliver, *"The Summer Day"*

Attention, taken to its highest degree,
    is the same thing as prayer.
        —Simone Weil, *Gravity and Grace*

Is there anything more important in this life than paying attention? Probably noticing the smell of the grass, the warmth of the sun on our face, or the whisper of our spouse is the best thing we can do with our life. Can we find anything that nurtures our marriage more than attention? We can all see that considering our spouse's needs, feelings, and dreams is essential. Does anything help us in our prayer life more than paying attention? Followers of the Christian contemplative tradition point out that attention is at the heart of prayer. Perhaps, as

Thomas Keating suggests, being watchful of God is the only activity that we engage in during Centering Prayer.[168] The rest is up to God.

Centering Prayer turns attention around. Most of us think of prayer as something we do to get God's attention. However, contemplative prayer is about giving God our attention.[169] This idea appears in the teachings of John of the Cross, who is quoted by Thomas Laird as saying, "Preserve a loving attentiveness to God with no desire to feel or understand any particular thing concerning God."[170] What a radical idea! This notion is about as extreme as asking Santa Claus what he wants for Christmas. When was the last time you saw a child do that?

Scientists are now finding that the kind of attention we develop during contemplative prayer is a very special kind of concentration—a form that has the potential to change our mind. What is attention? How do we use it to deliberately restrain the wandering mind and bring silence to the mind? How is it related to the principles of intention, awareness, and remembering? Is there a strategy for capturing a roving mind? Is it bad if the mind roams during prayer? These are the questions addressed in this chapter.

What is attention? This may seem like the place to start, but we actually need to introduce another concept first: *intention*. Neuroscientist Andrew Newberg defines intention as the object upon which we decide to focus.[171] Choosing an intention is the first step in contemplative prayer. Perhaps this is why Thomas Keating points out that Centering Prayer is not so much an exercise of attention as intention.[172] Our intention in contemplative prayer is God's presence and action within.

Rachel, who you met in chapter 7 along with her husband, David, had been practicing Centering Prayer for six weeks. She was beginning to understand the power of intention: "In the past, when I prayed, I was typically doing something else—showering, driving the car. Now, with this practice, I am simply trying to be present to one thing: God. I am not really trying to do anything other than show up. It is so nice to think that there is nothing else I need to do. I can simply be with God. Yes, sometimes I fall into the trap of wanting something special to happen . . . to feel peaceful, to have some type of experience. . . . But at other times, I let go of any expectations."

Now, we turn to attention. *Attention* is defined as the narrowing of our focus to our intention. Without an intention, we cannot have attention. Let me illustrate it this way. When I return home at night, wanting to unlock the front door, I need both an intention and attention. My intention—the focus of my attention—is the keyhole. I have to concentrate my attention on the keyhole in order to get inside. Understanding the importance of attention, someone came up with a key that has a built-in light. This really helps me focus my attention on my intention.

This very practical example of getting into my house illustrates the use of intention and attention, but according to the contemplative tradition, the same principles apply to getting into our inmost being. In Centering Prayer, our intention is to go inside where God dwells. And in prayer, we must focus our attention on this intention. We must concentrate on or watch our intention. A necessary part of praying is watching. On several occasions, Jesus said to "watch and pray" (Matthew 26:41; Mark 13:33). We must be alert to where our attention is.

Paying attention to our intention—God—requires entering into a mystery. The mystery is that we are turning our attention to something that the mind cannot comprehend. We are trying to focus on—or see—something that is in the dark. Perhaps this kind of attention is similar to the type I used as a child when I played hide-and-seek. I can remember my favorite hiding place—deep inside my mom's closet. I loved to close the door and push deep into the closet, behind all the long coats, up into the corner. In the dark, I couldn't see anything but I stayed alert. With my eyes wide open, I kept watch, listening for the sound of the one who was "it."

In contemplative prayer, we also pay attention in the dark. Darkness does not mean that our normal mental processes go blank.[173] It simply means that we are taking a break from the normal functions of the mind for a period of time. Instead of paying attention to the ordinary flow of our thoughts, we are aware that we are making ourselves present to God. With attention, we are alert to the one who is seeking us as we pray. With the same eager alertness that I had as a child playing hide-and-seek, we are watching and waiting for God to find us.

There is a fact that we must acknowledge as we attempt to focus our attention on God: our attention has a tendency to wander. Thoughts will continue to keep coming—memories, emotions, narratives—and we must just accept this as a fact.[174] If we realize our mind's tendency to wander, we will be less upset when thoughts arrive. On the other hand, if we think that the goal of contemplation is to be free of all thoughts, we are sure to be frustrated and disappointed.

Rachel found that her attention wandered during Centering Prayer—a common problem for anyone who meditates or practices contemplative prayer. When this happened, she had a tendency to be self-critical: "I sometimes berate myself when my attention wanders and say, 'Why can't you get rid of thoughts?' I can become judgmental and tell myself that I'm not cut out for this. I think, 'Maybe others can do this, but not you.' On a good day, though, I don't worry about the wandering and accept it as natural."

This is where the principle of awareness comes into play. *Awareness* is defined as noticing when our attention has wandered. In awareness forms of Christian contemplative prayer, we are instructed to stop and identify mental activities once they are noticed. For example, I would stop and make a note: "I was thinking about my plans for today. Memories of yesterday are on my mind. I am feeling afraid." However, since Centering Prayer is a surrendering form of contemplative prayer, we simply notice that a mental activity has captured our attention and let that thought go.

In a recent session with Rachel and David, Rachel described her experience with the awareness of wandering thoughts: "Sometimes, when my attention wanders, I catch it rather quickly. For example, I know that my to-do list is going to come up, so I am prepared for this. However, at other times, I can be deep in thought for who know how long before I become aware that my attention has wandered. For example, today during my Centering Prayer time, I was caught up in thinking about a difficult conversation between David and I. Without intending to, I was replaying the conversation, wondering what I should have said or done. I even found myself feeling angry all over again."

In Centering Prayer, what do we do when we become aware that our attention has wandered from our intention? This is where the principle of remembering comes in. *Remembering* is the process of returning our attention to our intention. Perhaps some thought has captured and turned our focus away from God. Now that we are aware that our attention has roamed, we remember to re-collect our attention and return it to our intention.

There are two guidelines in Centering Prayer that help us with these principles of intention, attention, awareness, and remembering. The first guideline is to "choose a sacred word as a symbol of your intention to consent to God's presence and action within."[175] A sacred word reminds us of our intention. What is a sacred word? Thomas Keating adopted the use of a sacred word from *The Cloud of Unknowing* which suggests, "If you want to gather this focus into one word, making it easier to grasp, select a little word of one syllable, not two. The shorter the word, the more it helps the work of the spirit. *God* or *love* works well."[176] Realizing that a word may not be effective for all practitioners, Keating offers the breath as a substitute if using a sacred word does not work for you.

It took awhile before Rachel settled on a sacred word: "When I first started, I chose the word *Jesus* as my sacred word. However, I found that word distracting, because when I would use it, my mind would begin to think of stories about Jesus. I moved on to words like *peace* and *trust,* but I found those words also distracting. In the last two weeks, I have settled on the word *yes.* This word reminds that I am simply surrendering to God. Saying 'yes' helps me let go of any thought as I return my attention to God."

When trying to describe a sacred word, it is probably easiest to explain what it is not. It is not a mantra, because a mantra is something that is repeated constantly as one engages in meditation.[177] In Centering Prayer, we only use the sacred word when we notice that our mind is attracted to a thought outside of our intention to be close to God. It is used as a reminder of our intention and it is employed as a way to turn away from or to let go of a thought. The second guideline is this: "When you become aware of a thought, return ever-so-gently to the sacred word."

Centering Prayer starts with an intention. Then, when our attention wanders, the sacred word is used to bring our attention back to our intention. I like the metaphor that Martin Laird offers for an intention. He says that intention is like an anchor line that tethers us and guides us back when our mind wanders.[178] An anchor line is used to attach a boat to a stationary device, such as an anchor or boat dock. The anchor line prevents the boat from drifting too far away from the object to which it is moored.

Our minds, like boats in the water and wind, are apt to drift. However, the sacred word acts as an anchor line. At some point, our mind will feel the tug of the sacred word reminding us that our attention has drifted from our original intention. Gently saying the sacred word will return our attention to our intention.

It is important to avoid the mistake of thinking that there is something wrong when our mind wanders. To help us with this idea, Cynthia Bourgeault tells the story of a conversation between a nun and Thomas Keating.[179] The nun, after sitting in Centering Prayer for twenty minutes, complains of being a failure because of ten thousand thoughts that she had during the time of prayer. Thomas Keating responds by saying, "How lovely! Ten thousand opportunities to return to God."[180] This story captures the essence of Centering Prayer because this is a practice based on remembering and returning our attention to our intention.

The skills of contemplative practice emerge from our proper responses to the distractions that we meet during our times of prayer. Will we judge ourselves harshly—"I'm doing it wrong!"—or will we look at the diversion as another opportunity to develop our attention? Will we think of our mind as something that we must control—"I must not have any thoughts!"—or will we be kind to the thoughts that emerge? When we are kind, we will say, "There's another thought. I must gently let it go." Our mind may or may not become silent during our time of prayer. That is not the goal. Our goal is to be open to God. Our goal is to aim and sustain our attention on God. The rest is up to Him.

Try this:

1. When you begin your time of Centering Prayer, take time to set your intention. In other words, remind yourself of why you have stopped to sit and pray. You are being present to God's presence and action within.

2. Before you begin your time of Centering Prayer, remind yourself that your mind will wander and that this is normal. It is not wrong or bad. Think of it as an opportunity to return your attention to God. Practice being kind to yourself when your attention wanders.

3. Settle on a sacred word before you begin your time of Centering Prayer. Avoid changing your word in the middle of your time of Centering Prayer. However, it is fine to try out another word during your next prayer time.

CHAPTER 11

Openness

This being human is a guest house.
Every morning a new arrival.

A joy, a depression, a meanness,
some momentary awareness comes
as an unexpected visitor.

Welcome and entertain them all!
Even if they're a crowd of sorrows,
who violently sweep your house
empty of its furniture,
still, treat each guest honorably.
He may be clearing you out
for some new delight.

The dark thought, the shame, the malice,
meet them at the door laughing,
and invite them in.

Be grateful for whoever comes,
because each has been sent
as a guide from beyond.
—Rumi, "The Guest House," translated by Coleman Barks

The contemplative life is a calling to the most
  vulnerable and critical openness.
                    —John O'Donohue, Beauty

Now that we have defined *what* attention is, it is time to raise another question: *How* do we pay attention? Centering Prayer teaches us that we pay attention with openness. *Openness* is defined as watchfulness of the present moment with acceptance. Let's examine the three different elements of openness: watchfulness, presence, and acceptance.

Watching is something with which we are all familiar. We usually think of watching as turning our attention out—as in, looking out. In ancient times, people erected watchtowers, a structure that created a high observation point. From this elevated place, they could be on the lookout for any threat or danger. However, in Centering Prayer, we are looking in. We are watching the activities that appear on the screen of our mind as we engage in contemplative prayer.

One of Thomas Keating's favorite metaphors for contemplative practice is comparing it to sitting on a riverbank watching the boats go by.[181] (The boats symbolize the thoughts that float by on the river of our mind.) As long as we sit on the bank, observing the boats as they float by, our attention will deepen. However, if we are captivated by a boat, and leave the riverbank to climb aboard the vessel, then we have diverted our attention from its intention.

Watchfulness is actually an ancient contemplative practice that refers to the process of awakening the witness within each of us.[182] Many of us begin the contemplative journey acknowledging how restless the mind is. However, we naïvely assume that our mind will be quickly tamed and that we will spend most of our time in contemplative prayer in a state of quiet bliss. Nothing could be further from the truth. Instead, much of our time in contemplative prayer involves watching or witnessing the appearance of a long line of mental visitors. During our period of prayer, instead of enjoying the peace of God, we may be greeted by upsetting memories, unpleasant emotions, and elaborate narratives. What is our attitude when these thoughts show up? (Thomas Keating uses the word "thought" to refer to any mental activity.)[183]

The first thing we must do when a thought shows up is to watch it.

This is more difficult than it sounds. Noticing a thought can be difficult because of the tendency of many mental activities to remain unconscious. A memory or emotion may be present during our time of Centering Prayer, but it might remain outside of our awareness. We faintly hear something mumbling, but the meaning is not clear. All we may initially sense is a vague, unpleasant physical sensation or restlessness.

Mental activities can be sneaky. When we are not alert and watching, they can capture our attention without our even knowing it. Perhaps this is the reason that Jesus instructs us to "watch and pray." There are times when I am deep in thought, and I think: "I'm supposed to be attending to my intention. When did my attention get captured? How long have I been lost in this thought?" Then, I use my sacred word to return my attention to God.

When I awaken the witness within me, I begin to watch myself watching the thought. The witness is that part of me which observes the mental visitors as they show up. The first visitor may be a memory of a past event. Hopefully, I observe myself observing this memory soon after it arrives. The watching is brief, because I use my sacred word to let go of the thought and return to my intention. Nevertheless, there is a fleeting moment of witnessing. Next, an unpleasant physical sensation or emotion appears. Again, I watch myself watching this unpleasant sensation, and again, the observing is momentary. But there is still a time of witnessing the watching.

Rachel's husband David, who was also practicing Centering Prayer, described his experience of being watchful: "In the past few weeks, I have become a better observer of my physical sensations, thoughts, and emotions. For example, just this morning during Centering Prayer, I was caught up in an imaginary conversation with Rachel. . . . I was planning what I was going to say to her about an issue we have been discussing. I noticed that my stomach had gotten tense, as I was lost in that thought. Once I became aware of the thought and tension, I used my sacred word to release the thought and to relax."

Watching, which occurs in the moment, leads us to the second element of openness: focusing on the present. How long does the present moment last? It is extremely short; perhaps three to four seconds—about as long as a breath cycle.[184] When we breathe in and out, that is a moment. Perhaps one reason why breathing has been central to the Christian contemplative tradition is because it keeps us positioned in the present moment.

Centering Prayer rests in the present moment—that is, "I am paying attention to God right now"—but the ordinary mind is uncomfortable with the present. The mind is attracted to the past and the future, but not the present. Therefore, during times of contemplative prayer, our mind can be captured by memories of the past or by thoughts of the future. As a result, we must repeatedly retrieve our attention from these time periods and return our focus to the present.

The final element of openness is acceptance. *Acceptance* is defined as bringing our attention back to our intention without judgment. This is difficult because the mind has a tendency to judge and evaluate things, which can show up in the form of judgmental thoughts about others. Perhaps a memory and an accompanying emotion surface during your time of contemplative prayer. Before you know it, you are weaving a judgmental story about a person from your past: "I can't believe how selfish that person was. I am so angry because of what that person did!" Your attention is not only captured by the memory or emotion, but it is also under the control of your judging narrative.

The tendency of the mind to judge also shows up in how we treat ourselves when we become aware that we have wandered from our intention: "You shouldn't be thinking or feeling that." Or, we may evaluate ourselves for not doing contemplative prayer the "right way." Our judgment may sound like this: "What is wrong with you? You are terrible at this. Other people do it better than you. You'll never get it right. You might as well give up."

Returning to the metaphor of boats on the river, because of our judgmental attitude, we may begin to judge the thoughts that float down the river of our mind. We may decide that some thoughts are bad so we reject them and try to push them aside. On the other hand, we may judge other thoughts as good and cling to them. They are attractive so we spend more time with them. Now, we are not only captured by the original thought, but we float even further away from our intention as we weave a story of judgment.

Let me illustrate with this example. I love to watch people. Sitting at my table, sipping a cup of tea, I watch as the people pass by. One person walks by and I get lost in a complimentary story: "He must be athletic. I bet he is successful. I like his jacket." However, as another person passes, I create a narrative about her flaws and weaknesses: "She doesn't take very good care of herself. I wonder if she ever exercises. She needs someone to teach her how to dress." Both types of stories are judgmental. However, on some occasions, people walk by and I don't make up a story. I just notice them without making any evaluations and return my attention to the nice cup of tea. This last response is an example of acceptance.

The goal in Centering Prayer is not to stop the thoughts that come down the sidewalk of our mind. We simply want to develop an accepting attitude toward them. This accepting attitude is reinforced through a simple formula called "The Four Rs":

Resist no thought
Retain no thought
React to no thought
Return to the sacred word[185]

As you attempt to lay aside your thoughts in prayer and create space for God, the complete opposite may happen.[186] At the psychological level, as we take an accepting stance toward our mental processes, our customary defenses against thoughts are lowered.[187] As we sit in contemplative prayer, things that we have not thought about for years, all sorts of repressed memories and distressing emotions, may come flooding into our awareness. In other words, the space gets filled with emotions and memories that have been hidden in the unconscious. This experience is referred to as an unloading of the unconscious. Thomas Keating writes, "This dynamism is a kind of divine psychotherapy, organically designed for each of us, to empty out our unconscious and free us from the obstacles to the free flow of grace in our minds, emotions, and bodies."[188] This experience can be peaceful at times and frightening at other times. Nevertheless, they are both part of the process of healing that occurs during contemplative prayer.

Up to this point, we have examined Centering Prayer as a formal practice, a time for sitting and following the four guidelines. However, Thomas Keating insists on working the effects of contemplative prayer into our daily lives.[189] As a result, we go from practicing Centering Prayer to realizing a centered life. In addition to watching memories as they appear during our time of prayer, we observe them as they arise during a disagreement with our spouse. Just as we attempt to catch a narrative the moment it surfaces during Centering Prayer, we try to notice the story as soon as it shows up in response to a disappointment at home. And finally, not only do we see emotions as they arise while engaged in our practice of contemplative prayer, we also pay attention to the feelings triggered by an unpleasant event.

How do we go from paying attention with openness during Centering Prayer to extending openness into our daily life? To help us address this question, we will turn to the Welcoming Prayer—developed by Mary Mrozowski, one of Keating's closest associates—for guidance.[190] It is important to point out that the Welcoming Prayer is designed for working with one specific, yet crucial, mental function: emotions. Of course, how we deal with emotions is extremely critical to our personal and interpersonal well-being.

The first two steps of the Welcoming Prayer are:

1. Focus and sink in
2. Welcome

In the first step, we feel the emotion as a sensation in our body. Instead of immediately letting the emotion go, as we do in Centering Prayer, we allow ourselves to pay attention to the feeling. We become aware of how the energy of the emotion shows up as a physical sensation at that moment. For example, if the emotion is fear, focus on the sensation of fear. Are you short of breath? Do you feel a surge of energy? Don't try to change anything. Avoid falling into commentaries on the emotion, such as: "I am being mistreated. No one will ever listen to me. This feeling is unbearable. I must find a way to escape this feeling." Just stay present to the physical sensations.

David described his experience with feeling emotions as sensations in his body: "I am getting better at noticing when my stomach gets tight or my jaw clenches. I don't try to change the sensations as much as just notice them. I allow the tension to be there and observe it. In the past, I would have acted upon those physical sensations, but now, I am learning to make room for the tension."

The second step is to welcome the emotion. Begin to say to yourself, ever so gently, "Welcome, fear" (or whatever the emotion is). You may be thinking, "Aren't we trying to get rid of the emotion?" The answer is no. At this point, we are not attempting to let go of the emotion, as we would if we were practicing Centering Prayer. As we welcome the feeling in our daily life, we are trying to create an atmosphere of inner hospitality. There is no judgment or rejection of the emotion; there is simply openness. We are not judging it by saying that the emotion is bad or wrong. We are not accusing ourselves for having the emotion. Instead, we are accepting it, and by welcoming it, we disarm it and reduce its harmful effects.

David was learning to welcome his emotions. He told this story one day during our session: "I asked Rachel to go a concert with me but she couldn't because of a deadline at work. A little while later, I noticed that my posture had slumped and my chest felt heavy. 'What was I feeling?' I must be feeling sad. So, I just allowed myself to feel the sadness.

Instead of thinking it was wrong to be sad or trying to get rid of it, I just allowed the sadness to be there. After awhile, I noticed that the sadness had decided to leave. I really wanted to go to the concert, so I asked a good friend to go with me."

This second step of the Welcoming Prayer returns us full circle to the poem with which we began this chapter. As Rumi notes in his poem "The Guest House," emotions may show up in our daily life as unexpected visitors. We may be surprised by their presence, but we still offer them hospitality. We welcome them, entertain them, and treat them as honorable guests, because inviting them in may be clearing us out "for some new delight." I like to think that this "new delight" is God's presence. By opening ourselves to emotions, memories, and thoughts, we may be able to see that "there is something utterly vast and sacred already within us, this silent land that runs deeper than these obsessive mental patterns."[191]

Try this:

1. During Centering Prayer, think of your thoughts as boats floating by on a river. See if you can watch the thoughts as they show up, and then just let them pass by.

2. Can you watch yourself watching thoughts, physical sensations, or emotions as they show up on the screen of your mind? For example, when you feel a spot on your face itching, resist the urge to scratch it. Instead, watch yourself watching the itchy place.

3. For one breath cycle (one inhalation and one exhalation), pay attention to the screen of your mind. Does any thought show up during that one moment in time? Watch how you respond to that thought.

4. Does any judgment show up during your time of Centering Prayer? Do you get caught up in judgmental thoughts about others, or do you judge yourself for not being good at Centering Prayer? If so, return to your sacred word and release the judgmental thought.

5. Catch an emotion as it shows up in the form of physical sensation. First, pay attention to the sensations. Make space for them and allow them to be present. Then, welcome the emotion that accompanies the physical sensation. You are not judging it or rejecting it. You are just allowing it to be present.

CHAPTER 12

Letting Go

Adopt the attitude that was in Christ Jesus:
Though he was in the form of God,
he did not consider being equal with God something to exploit.
But he emptied himself
by taking the form of a slave
and by becoming like human beings.
When he found himself in the form of a human,
he humbled himself by becoming obedient to the point of death,
even death on a cross.

—Philippians 2:5–8

Centering prayer is an exercise in letting go. That is all it is.
—Thomas Keating, Open Mind, Open Heart

Thomas Keating boils Centering Prayer down to one exercise: letting go.[192] Within the Christian tradition, letting go has a long history, because when we let go, we are following the example set for us by Jesus, who "emptied himself" (Philippians 2:7). In addition to describing letting go as emptying, the contemplative tradition also uses terms such as dying, detachment, and surrender. In this chapter, we will examine all of these concepts in an effort to get to the core skill of contemplative prayer: letting go.

What did the writer of Philippians mean when he said that Jesus emptied himself? The Christian contemplative tradition claims that Jesus was no longer laying claim to his identity as God.[193] No longer would he simply be God. Instead, he was accepting another identity, that of a human being. Our contemplative journey is the same—emptying ourselves of one identity so that we may take on another.

The Christian contemplative tradition asserts that we cling to an identity that we call a "self." However, we have been duped into thinking that this is our true identity.[194] There is a smaller self and there is a larger Self, and the smaller self acts as an imposter. In other words, the smaller self claims to be our true self. According to Thomas Keating, mistaking the small self for the large Self is the disease of the human condition.[195]

After several weeks of practicing Centering Prayer, Kevin from chapter 2 was beginning to recognize the small self. He described it this way: "Sometimes, I have a tendency to focus on the differences between myself and [his wife] Stephanie. I find myself thinking about how I do things the right way, while she does things the wrong way. I can find myself feeling responsible for getting things to happen in a certain way . . . the way I want. I start thinking that I need to fix things. To me, these are indicators of the small self."

The contemplative tradition not only claims that we must empty ourselves of this small or false self, but teaches us how to do it through contemplative prayer. In prayer, we learn to relieve the small self of its vital roles. What are the functions of the self? First, as it observes and describes the mental activities of the mind, the self provides us with a sense of knowing. This knowing comes with a sense that "I am my thoughts, memories, and feelings." Second, it authors a narrative of our lives, putting ourselves in the center. Locating ourselves at the center of a narrative comes with certain dangers. One hazard is that our own thoughts and feelings become more important than those of others. Another threat is that we can imbue our stories with a sense of certainty or authority. In other words, our version of events is the authorized or "right" version.

Through contemplative prayer we empty or relieve the self of its duties. How do we do this? By laying aside or letting go of every thought. In Centering Prayer, when a thought appears, we do not give it the attention that the self wants to offer it. We acknowledge it, but then by using our sacred word, we gently return our attention to our intention. By not giving the thought attention, we are removing support from under the self. Imagine the self sitting upon a three-legged stool. The legs are memories, emotions, and narratives. By removing the legs of the stool, the self is indirectly dethroned.

Scripture describes this adventure of emptying in several ways. For example, John the Baptist uses the metaphor of a wedding party to capture the experience of letting go (John 3:29). If Jesus is the groom, John refers to himself as the groom's friend. And as the groom's friend he has to let go of what he might think, want, or feel at the wedding. His wants just aren't that important. John the Baptist expresses the experience of emptying this way: "He must increase and I must decrease" (John 3:30).

Kevin was also learning to let go of what he thought, wanted, and felt. He said, "Before I started Centering Prayer, I had to be in charge. I assumed that my way of doing things was the right way. But learning to let go of my thoughts has helped me learn how to let go of my way of doing things. Now, I am more willing to come up with a shared product. Now, I know that the world spins without me."

Jesus uses the metaphor of a seed to express the meaning of emptying or dying: "I assure you that unless a grain of wheat falls into the earth and dies, it can only be a single seed. But if it dies, it bears much fruit" (John 12:24). When we empty our thoughts in Centering Prayer, it seems as if the self is dying. Another way to put it is that the self has lost its central role. The self understandably feels threatened and frightened by this proposal. Think about it this way—how would you feel if you lost your job? You would probably feel like a part of you had died.

Thomas Merton calls this a revolution that turns everything completely around.[196] This is a violent revolution, one that calls for the death of the person you have come to think of as your self. However, this death is necessary if there is going to be new life. The one seed must fall into the ground and die in order to give birth to a stalk with innumerable seeds. The false self must die in order for the larger Self to be born.

In contemplative prayer, therefore, we let go of the self by emptying the mind. This process can be compared to letting water out of the bathtub.[197] We don't have to *push* water out of the tub. Thanks to gravity, all we have to do is remove the stopper and the water simply runs out by itself. We are doing the same thing in contemplative prayer. We simply allow the thoughts to flow out of us.

However, letting go of thoughts is counterintuitive. During our lifetime, we have become dependent on thinking. Our natural tendency is to cling to or grasp the contents of our mind. This reminds me of a story I heard about the monkey and the coconut. According to this story, villagers in a far-off land wanted to capture monkeys. One smart person thought of cutting a hole in a coconut and stuffing peanuts into it. Soon thereafter, a monkey approached the coconut, smelled the peanuts, and put his hand inside the coconut. When the villagers approached, the monkey could easily have escaped if it had released the peanuts, extracted its hand from the coconut, and run away. However, because the monkey would not let go of the peanuts, its hand was stuck. As a result, it was captured. We are like the monkey. We are attracted to a thought that comes along, and so we cling to it. However, our freedom is dependent on letting go of the thought.

Over time, Kevin had become more aware of his tendency to cling to certain thoughts: "I notice that I am clinging to something when my stomach seems twisted up or tight. When I stop to notice this, I become aware that I am clinging to a certain desire or expectation. I am thinking that things around me have to be a certain way, or I am wanting Stephanie to act in a certain way. If these thoughts come up during my time of Centering Prayer, and they do, I am learning to just let them go."

Clinging to or rejecting a thought usually appears in the form of a narrative. If we find a thought appealing, we create a positive account that keeps us attached to that mental activity. On the other hand, if the mental process is unpleasant, we create a negative story about that thought. The narratives seem very different, but they have the same undesirable outcome. They keep us trapped in our mental activities. Freedom comes about as we adhere to the Four Rs of Centering Prayer: resist no thought, retain no thought, react to no thought, and return to the sacred word.[198] Before we can become attached to the memory or emotion with a positive or negative story, we let the thought go by returning to the sacred word and to our intention.

According to the contemplative tradition, prayer is detachment from ordinary mental processes. This is important because our attachment to thoughts upsets the balance of our minds.[199] Attachment creates two fundamental problems. First, it creates a desire. Instead of simply having a thought, we cling to it. For example, if I become attached to the thought that my spouse must act a certain way, I may create a story of why this desire is reasonable and essential. Second, attachment causes distorted perceptions. Instead of seeing a thought as simply a creation of our mind, we begin to see it as real. For example, when my mind produces a thought of fear, instead of seeing the fear as a creation of my mind, I see it as a fact.

Some people have the assumption that contemplative prayer is the absence of thoughts—but this is not the case. Instead, the contemplative tradition teaches us to be detached from thoughts. David Benner quotes the fourth-century Desert Father Evagrius Ponticus: "Prayer is the laying aside of thoughts."[200] Thoughts will float down the river of our mind, and that is okay. Our instruction is to simply let the thought pass. Observe them, but do not engage—do not climb aboard the boat and turn your thoughts into a story. Instead, let them go.

This skill of observing thoughts and letting them go has been called *vigilance*.[201] Ancient contemplatives identified three elements of vigilance. First, meet the thought with stillness. Second, allow the thought to be present; don't try to drive it away. Finally, let go of the thought.

This description of vigilance reminds me of the Welcoming Prayer.[202] The Welcoming Prayer is the means by which we bring the Centering Prayer into our daily lives. The Welcoming Prayer, which focuses on the emotions that emerge during the day, has three steps: focus and sink in, welcome, and let go. In step one, we meet the feeling. In step two, we allow it to be present. After spending sufficient time going back and forth between steps one and two, we move on to the final step: let it go. We don't push the emotion away prematurely. However, when the emotion begins to dissolve of its own accord, we let it go.

With time, Centering Prayer was helping Kevin learn how to let go of his anger toward Stephanie. He described the process this way: "Because I was trained as a child to be a peacekeeper, I often have focused more upon Stephanie's emotions than my own. However, I am now more aware of my feelings. I have learned that I can't let go of my emotions if I'm not aware of their presence. Instead of judging myself for having anger, I am getting better at making room for it."

Earlier, we learned that there are two major types of Christian contemplative prayer, awareness and surrender, and that Centering Prayer falls into the second category of surrender. The body has its own language for surrendering: putting one's hands up with palms wide open. This body language assures the captor that the surrendering person does not hold a weapon in his or her hands. In order to surrender, one must let go of that which he or she is hanging onto.

The struggle to relinquish that to which one has been clinging is captured in a song written by BarlowGirl entitled "Surrender." The lyrics describe a person who has been asked to relinquish her ideas of who she is. She laments that she "can't open my hands, can't let go." Letting go of something that she has spent so long forming and fashioning—her identity—is hard to do. But a gentle voice replies that the act of surrender will set her free.

This song captures both the fear and hope of surrendering. Letting go of our thoughts is frightful because we identify with them; we think these thoughts are our self. What will it be like to be empty? The hope of surrendering is freedom. We will be free to find out what is behind all our normal mental activities. We will be free to find a new Self. We will be free to find out what we can be filled with when we are empty of ourselves. We will be free to discover a new attitude.

Try this:

1. Try to be more aware of the small self and the large Self. What are the indicators for you that the small self is active? Are you trying to fix or control the situation? Do you notice when the large Self shows up? Perhaps you are listening more, or offering more choices to your spouse.

2. Notice how your mind responds to the practice of letting go of thoughts. Does it keep trying to sneak in a new thought? Does it tell you that your practice is boring, or a waste of time? Does it invite you to do something "more important"?

3. Notice how you cling to certain thoughts and resist others during your time of Centering Prayer. When you are clinging to a thought, you probably think about it for a while before you even notice it. When you resist it, you probably feel a dislike for the thought and want to get rid of it quickly. Using the metaphor of draining water out of the bathtub, try to allow your thoughts to leave your consciousness smoothly, effortlessly, like water flowing down a drain.

4. Notice a painful emotion this week. Avoid the tendency to judge and reject it. Instead, watch it as it naturally rises and then falls away. Welcome it, spend some time with it, and then allow it to leave.

CHAPTER 13

Union

Divine union is the goal of all Christians.
— *Thomas Keating, Open Mind, Open Heart*

*My prayer is . . . that all of them may be one, Father,
just as you are in me and I am in you.*
— *John 17: 20–21*

You have probably heard the popular expression, "I'm so into you." If you were unfamiliar with our modern culture, you might think that this phrase is referring to a strong sense of unity between two people. However, this saying falls short of this meaning. The expression simply means that one person is attracted to someone else in a romantic way. At some level, we want to feel connected because it provides us with a sense of safety and security and it stabilizes our mind. However, we conclude that this feeling of unity is hard—if not impossible—to grasp and hold on to. We want closeness, but all too often we seem to find ourselves feeling alone and separate, a state that leaves our mind out of balance.

We are back to where we began our journey into minds and marriages. That is, we have returned to the concepts of separation and union. We want to feel connected to someone. We want to experience the oneness that Jesus prayed for in John 17, but instead, we feel an unwanted gap between ourselves and others. Where does this sense of separation originate? What is this union that Jesus prayed for? How can contemplative prayer bring us to a place of connection, and what can we expect once we get there?

The Christian contemplative tradition teaches us that this sense of separation from God and others is the human condition.[203] As John O'Donohue says, "Our minds constantly insist on seeing walls of separation."[204] Our mind believes a lie: that we are over here and that God—or our spouse—is over there. This perception of separation is a result of our memories, emotions, and narratives. And as long as these activities of the mind imprison us, the gap between us appears as a vast chasm.

The Christian contemplative tradition exposes this lie. The contemplatives teach us that when our mind is telling us that God is far away, we are "not even inches away from the divine presence."[205] The wall of separation is actually a veil. God is as close to us as our next breath, and following the path of contemplative prayer will lead us to this divine union.

Centering Prayer is a process of letting go of the activities of the mind, because it is this noise in our mind that creates the illusion of separateness from God. We learn to bring silence to our mind by bringing stillness to our body, by focusing our attention on our intention of God, by noticing distracting thoughts, and by letting go of these mental activities. Practicing the skills of Centering Prayer allows our mind to settle down, to become quiet. When the functions of the mind seem to cease and our mind becomes silent, the veil of separation parts and we enter into God's presence.

The truth is that we do not have to do anything to enter into union with God. The contemplatives teach us that we are already in God's presence. We are already there, we just don't know it yet. Union with God is not something that we have to work at or acquire. It would be strange if someone said, "I need to work at breathing." No, we don't work at it, because it is already happening on its own. We simply need to become aware of it, and accept it. As John O'Donohue writes, "Perhaps the secret of spiritual integrity has to do with an act of acceptance, namely, a recognition that you are always already within the divine embrace."[206]

Union does come with a price, however: the death of the small self. This sounds like a strange payment because we are so invested in this element of the mind called the self. It takes a long time to build a sense of "this is who I am," with thoughts and feelings that distinguish you from everyone else. You have gotten used to commenting on the contents of your mind. What you think, feel, and remember seems very personal. The contents of your mind—emotions, memories, narratives, and decisions to act—belong to you only, no one else. It seems important to protect this thing called self, so this idea of death sounds very threatening.

This is where the practice of letting go during Centering Prayer comes in. In contemplative prayer, we learn to relieve the self of its roles. We learn to quit paying attention to the feelings, memories, thoughts, and stories in our mind. Maybe I don't need to know what is going on in my mind. Could it be that these mental processes are not that important? Maybe I can let go of the actions of my mind without reflecting or commenting on them.

As we let go of the small self, an amazing truth presents itself. Gerald May identifies the discovery this way: "When self-definition is momentarily suspended and self-image fades from the foreground, the true self remains."[207] Come to find out, there is something behind the small self: the true Self. The true Self is the gift of "the being that God has given us with its transcendent potential."[208] At this spiritual level of our being, where we access the unique identity that God intends for us, we gain entrance into our immense possibilities and our goodness. Thomas Merton describes the emergence of the true Self as the awakening of the unknown I "that is beyond observation and reflection and is incapable of commenting upon itself."[209] This real Self is a mystery that lies beyond words.

At this point, when the mind becomes quiet and the small self fades into the background, union with God is possible. Thomas Keating puts it this way, "This is what divine union is. There is no reflection of self."[210] By finding our true Self, we discover God; and by encountering God, we find out who we are in God.[211] In the words of Saint Augustine, "May I know you, may I know myself."[212] During this time of knowing, during this time of union, we are being transformed.

How can we describe this experience of union with God if we are not supposed to be aware of it as it is happening? First, this encounter with God usually comes as a feeling of completion or well-being. Next, we can say that it is typically brief, lasting perhaps only an instant. According to Thomas Keating, "It only takes a moment for God to enrich you."[213] Finally, it is a time devoid of thoughts. For a while, the mind is silent. During this short period, our ordinary way of viewing the world, time, or even ourselves simply falls by the wayside as we enter into a deeper dimension of ourselves.

Ultimately, divine union is a gift. We cannot work to achieve it. Actually, it happens when we are not trying to do anything, control anything, or accomplish anything.[214] The experience comes by doing less. Contemplative prayer is about letting go.

Steve and Linda, the couple we met in the introduction, both decided to practice Centering Prayer. On a few occasions, they each experienced a sense of union with God. Steve put his experience this way: "It felt similar to how I feel when I sit alone at night on the shore beside the ocean. I felt like I was part of something immense. It was like I was being absorbed into something much bigger than myself. I felt very connected to God. It was like losing myself in that moment with God."

Linda had another way of describing her experience of union: "It felt like I was sinking into something very peaceful. It felt very personal, like I was being held close. I don't know how much time passed because I had no sense of time. It was as if I was no longer there. I guess this is what people mean when they report a loss of self."

Once this experience of God's presence happens, our natural tendency is to try to hang on to it, but this is the biggest obstacle to union with God.[215] Of course we want to hold on to this experience, because for a fleeting moment, the illusion of separateness was lifted. For an instant, we were aware of the reality of our connection with God. But we can't hold on to God's presence. That is like trying to hold on to the wind. We can't create this divine union or recreate this experience of God's presence. It is simply a gift that we cannot manufacture or control. Centering Prayer is an exercise in letting go of everything.

After this moment of oneness with God dissipates, what do we do next? As this experience of union passes, we simply return to our customary way of experiencing ourselves. However, we do so with an appreciation for the hidden presence of God in the events of our daily lives. For example, when our spouse suggests that we do something different today, we wonder if God is at work. When things don't work out the way we planned, we look for something good in the altered situation. When our spouse responds in kindness to our need, we notice God's hand in their action. As James Finley, the psychologist and Christian contemplative, says, we return to our daily lives with a "renewed willingness."[216] Willingness is the opposite of trying to master, direct, and control our lives. Instead, it is a desire to say "yes to the mystery of being alive in each moment."[217]

Both Steve and Linda reported that their times of union with God had an impact on how they experienced their lives. Linda expressed it this way: "After experiencing union with God, I feel more connected to others and share their feelings more intensely. If they hurt, I feel their pain. If they are happy, it gives me great pleasure. I suppose you could say that I am better at coming alongside others as they experience the ups and downs of their lives."

Steve described it another way: "I feel a weight has been lifted. I don't feel so much like I have to fix everything or that the buck stops with me. I feel more confident. I feel assured that I am loved and not alone. I don't ever feel totally alone anymore like I used to."

One of the mysteries that we must be willing to enter into is the union of marriage. In his letter to the Christians in Ephesus, Paul wrote, "For this reason a man will leave his father and mother and be united to his wife, and the two will become one flesh. This is a profound mystery" (Ephesians 5:31–32). This mystery of oneness precludes an attitude of separateness. No longer can you maintain the illusion that there is a distance between your spouse and you. Paul makes this clear when he says that loving your spouse is an act of loving yourself (Ephesians 5:28). The wall between self and other seems to come down.

Steve agreed that his experience of union with God had affected his perceptions of marriage: "Sometimes now, I am less focused on Linda and myself as separate people. Instead, I am more aware of the connection between us. The experience of oneness with God leads me to take less credit for the successes in our relationship. It is almost like we are participating in something bigger than us that is orchestrating everything."

Perhaps it would serve us well to revive this ancient notion that marriage is a union. We are linked or attached to each other. What takes place in my mind affects my spouse and vice versa. And because we are connected in some mysterious way, how I treat my spouse affects me. The flow goes back and forth continuously. The linkage between us never stops. This belief mandates that marriage partners are responsible for each other. In part III, we will examine how to become experts in the care and treatment of each other. However, before turning to this subject, let's examine the love that is cultivated through contemplative prayer and the experience of divine union.

Try this:

1. Before beginning your time of Centering Prayer, remind yourself of what you can and cannot control. You cannot create an experience of union with God, because that is a gift. You cannot control your thoughts. However, you can choose to use your sacred word to

release all the thoughts that show up, which opens your heart to the possibility of having a union with God.

2. Remember that union with God is not the intent of your prayer. It is a gift from God, not something that you can create. At the end of your time of Centering Prayer, even if you did not have an experience of union with God, remind yourself that you were still in God's presence.

3. Notice if there are times this week when you have a "renewed willingness." In other words, times when you are less focused on directing and controlling your life or the lives of others. Make an effort to be more open to the mystery of how God is directing your day and intervening in your life.

4. Pay more attention this week to the ways in which you and your spouse are connected. Notice how you are affected by what your spouse says about you. Be observant of how your emotions impact your spouse's feelings. Pay attention to how you respond to your spouse's posture.

CHAPTER 14

Love

*Returning to the ultimate reality is the ultimate source
of security, love, and freedom.*
  —*Thomas Keating, The Mind's Own Physician*

Perfect love casts out fear.

  —*1 John 4:18*

The mind is designed to be powered by love. Fueled by compassion, the mind functions at its highest capacity. However, as we have discovered, the mind can also run on the power of fear. Under the control of fear, the mind quickly accesses memories, reflects on events, and makes decisions. The fearful mind appears to be doing its job of protecting us and determining appropriate courses of action, so we may not stop and ask: "How would my mind be functioning if it were powered by love?"

It's too bad that, at birth, we don't come with an owner's manual that provides us with these instructions: If your mind isn't working well off of fear, switch to love. When I recently purchased a Volkswagen, I read the owner's manual because I wanted to know what kind of gasoline the car ran on. Come to find out, buying the correct grade of gasoline was very important in order to prevent possible engine damage and loss of engine performance. The manual made it clear that my engine would definitely not function well if I tried to run it on a fuel with an octane rating below 87.

Just as it is feasible to operate a car engine on an inferior grade of gasoline, it is possible to power the mind with a harmful kind of fuel: fear. Let's review what happens when the mind runs on fear. When something happens to undermine our need for security, the threat response system is triggered and fear is our most basic reaction. Fear, garnering the support of the body and other properties of the mind—self, memories, and narratives—motivates us to act in ways that "appear" to protect the self. All the while, the fear-dominated mind is sabotaging our most important relationship.

The mind can operate under the influence of either fear or love, but not both. Findings from modern neuroscience teach us that the mind works in terms of patterns. If one system is turned on, then the other one will be switched off. One process negates the other. Fear will turn off the power of love or love will cancel the power of fear. The ancient author of 1 John had insight into this feature of the mind when he wrote, "Perfect love casts out fear" (1 John 4:18).

Love has the power to change how our mind operates; it is the antidote to fear. As Thomas Merton writes, "For only love . . . can exorcise the fear which is at the root of all war."[218] However, not just any kind of love will do. It must be "perfect" love. What kind of love is this? Where do we find it? What are the barriers to accessing it? How does a love-dominated mind function? We will turn to the Christian contemplative tradition for insight into these issues.

Love is not easily understood. I like James Thurber's definition of love: "Love is that pleasant confusion we know exists."[219] I like this definition because it gets at the mystery of love. As with all things of the Spirit, the logical mind cannot quite grasp the meaning of love. We can prepare an environment in which love can take root and grow. We can describe it when it blooms. However, love evades our efforts to define it.

Perhaps love is a puzzle because its source is a mystery. Where does love come from? We are confused on this issue, so as a result, we look in all the wrong places. Primarily, we turn to other people in our search for love. We turn to friends, family, and our spouse. We hope that their love can provide us with the safety and security we so desperately long for. However, love that comes from people is conditional. Inevitably, we have experiences of being criticized, disconnected, and unwanted by our loved ones. This, once again, arouses our deepest fears.

The mystery of love is that it is found within. John O'Donohue writes, "You can search for long years in lonely places, far outside yourself. Yet the whole time, this love is but a few inches away from you. It is at the edge of your soul, but you have been blind to its presence."[220] Jesus expressed this same idea in a conversation he had with a woman from Samaria (John 4: 7–13). He pointed out that she could ask for water from others, but that she would eventually get thirsty again. However, if she asked him for water, it would spring up from within. This is the nature of love; it flows from the inside. It cannot be conjured or worked up. It simply flows from a well within.

After several weeks of practicing Centering Prayer, Linda was beginning to notice a change in herself: "I am becoming less dependent on what Steve thinks about me. I am not trying so hard to prove myself to him or earn his love. Instead, I am beginning to notice a wonderful change. I am becoming more loving toward myself. It feels like love from the inside. I am definitely not so hard on myself."

The Christian contemplatives tell us that love is present and available, but something is blocking its flow. What is it? First, we are not free to love because we are prisoners of a noisy mind. We are locked within a narrow view of reality, a view that is focused on what I think, remember, feel, and want. In other words, we are restricted by the functions of our ordinary mind. Since we cannot get outside of our mind, we can only see our spouse and ourselves from this limiting perspective.

And at the center of this noisy mind is the self. The small self is busy monitoring the functions of the mind. It is constantly alert to feelings and thoughts, and it concludes, "I am these thoughts and emotions." The self is perpetually evaluating your environment, asking, "Am I safe? Am I in danger?" The small self is primarily focused on your safety and protection. But as Richard Rohr says, "We'll never see the love we really are, our foundation, if we keep living out of our false self of self-protection and overreaction."[221]

The hope offered by the Christian contemplative tradition is that freedom is possible. We can be liberated from the mental prison governed by fear and self. Through Centering Prayer, the noisy functions of the mind—remembering, feeling, and narrating—grow silent. Through the practice of letting go, the small self fades into the background.

When these changes occur—when we are liberated from our mental prisons—we are free to love. As John O'Donohue points out, "All your barriers are down."[222] As we let go of our small views of our spouse and ourselves, we begin to see the world through different eyes, the eyes of love. As we let go and forget about the self, we are free to love others. John O'Donohue adds, "Love begins . . . with an act of gracious self-forgetting."[223] In silence, unshackled from the noisy mind, untied from the small self, we are free to love.

Linda reported an unexpected result of Centering Prayer: "Things are less about me now. I am less apt to have my feelings hurt if Steve doesn't follow my advice and I am not so quick to get defensive if he says something that sounds critical. I let him know what I think, but I am less attached to things going my way. I guess you could say I'm more flexible. I'm sure he is glad that I am not so determined to convince him that I am perfect."

When we turn to God for love, we find security. The notion that security comes from the love of God is an ancient contemplative notion that modern science is beginning to discover. Perhaps Albert Einstein was the first modern scientist to catch a glimpse of this truth. He recognized our state of captivity to the limited capacities of the ordinary mind. He argued that our task is to free ourselves from this prison through widening our circle of love. Referring to these goals, Einstein said, "Nobody is able to achieve this completely, but the striving for such achievement is in itself a part of the liberation and a foundation for inner security."[224] In other words, security comes from within as we achieve freedom from the ordinary workings of the mind so that we are free to love.

Modern psychology—particularly findings from attachment theory—is discovering that a person can be freed from a past of insecurity. Researchers are finding that people who were insecure as children can overcome the limits of their history and achieve an "earned security." David Wallin, a psychologist who specializes in the integration of attachment theory and contemplative practices, points out that a regular contemplative practice can produce the same benefits as secure childhood attachments. He argues that through contemplative practice a person can generate an "internalized secure base."[225]

Linda said some things that let me know she was becoming more secure: "I don't have to convince Steve that I am a good person. Of course, I'm not perfect, but now I know that I am a good person. I don't have to prove myself to him anymore or work to earn his approval. In some ways, I feel more safe. Safety is like making it around the bases in a softball game. When I reach home base, I know that I am safe, or secure. There's no more anxiety or worry. The trip is finished."

In an effort to apply the attachment model to Christian contemplative prayer, psychologists Pehr Granqvist and Lee A. Kirkpatrick point out that an attachment figure provides several benefits.[226] The first is close proximity. Just as a child forms a secure attachment with a parent who maintains closeness, contemplative prayer helps practitioners experience a sense of God's nearness. In addition, the awareness of God's protection, support, and comfort during times of Centering Prayer provides a secure base. Over time, the benefits of contemplative practice translate into an earned security.

Granqvist and Kirkpatrick, in agreement with Christian contemplatives, argue that God is an entirely adequate attachment figure.[227] They contend that God is a protective and caring parent who is always reliable and available. This is the point that Thomas Keating makes when he says that the essence of the Christian contemplative tradition is the experience that Jesus had of God as *Abba*.[228] The Aramaic word Abba, roughly meaning "daddy," is an affectionate term that children use for a tender, loving father. For some people, the image of God-as-Father may not be appealing because of troubling relationships they had with their own fathers. Perhaps their fathers were judgmental, harsh, and unkind. If this was your experience, contemplative prayer holds out the hope that you can have a new experience with your heavenly father, one that is full of love.

Clearly, love and security are what the ordinary mind and self have so desperately wanted all along. We've just been looking in the wrong places. The Christian contemplative tradition tells us that love can be accessed through contemplative prayer, and this love brings with it an inner security. In this state of security, fueled by divine love, the mind becomes balanced. Once it is balanced, the mind can function at its highest capacity.

Try this:

1. Pay attention this week when your mind is under the influence of fear. In this mental state, what memories surface? What seems at the forefront of your thinking? What is your narrative about yourself or others involved? How do you behave? Notice if love has been turned off.

2. Notice a time this week when you are seeking the love of your spouse. What has triggered this motivation for your partner's love? Are you reacting to a perception that your spouse is distant, displeased, critical, etc.? Are you feeling like you have to prove yourself, or earn points, with your spouse?

3. Notice a time this week when you find security on the inside. In other words, a time when you feel like you are a good person just the way you are, and you don't feel a need to do something to earn your spouse's love. You feel like being yourself is good enough. You don't react to criticism or negativity coming from your spouse.

PART III

Transforming Your Marriage

CHAPTER 15

The Science of Contemplation

*I deeply welcome the invitation to participate in
a deep dialogue with science.*
—*Thomas Keating, The Mind's Own Physician*

Let's review our journey so far. In part I, with insights from modern scientists and Christian contemplatives, we sought to increase our understanding of the human mind. We explored how marital problems occur when the mind gets out of balance. Part II was based on the assumption that we can restore stability to the mind through contemplative prayer. Appealing to a rich Christian contemplative heritage, we identified how Centering Prayer cultivates certain mental skills. Now, in part III, it is time to ask the question: How can Centering Prayer benefit our marriage?

For insight into this question, we must turn to science. For almost four hundred years, science was not that interested in the study of the mind or the study of contemplative practices. This has changed dramatically in the past three decades, as research is beginning to show that contemplative practices not only balance our mind, but help us cultivate traits that can benefit our marital relationship. Science is now extremely interested in contemplative practices, how these practices affect the mind, and how contemplative methods can be applied in clinical settings that deal with physical and mental health. Scientists want to know how we can use contemplative methods to improve personal and interpersonal well-being.

The most recent scientific research is focused on a contemplative practice within Buddhism called mindfulness. Today, there are hundreds of research papers on the impact of mindfulness-based interventions on physical and mental conditions.[229] Currently, the National Institutes of Health (NIH) is funding almost forty different studies on the effectiveness of mindfulness-based treatments.

Why is the scientific community so interested in this contemplative practice called mindfulness? To answer this question, let's look at the influence of three men: Jon Kabat-Zinn, Richard Davidson, and the Dalai Lama. The pioneer in establishing mindfulness as a secular discipline is Jon Kabat-Zinn, a professor of medicine emeritus at the University of Massachusetts.[230] In 1979, he created a program called Mindfulness-Based Stress Reduction (MBSR) to help patients cope with chronic pain and disease. In 1990, Kabat-Zinn put out his first book, *Full Catastrophe Living*, which contained a detailed description of the routine he taught in his stress-reduction clinic at UMass.[231] Today, MBSR programs taught by certified MBSR teachers exist in more than five hundred hospitals and clinics. More than eighteen thousand people have taken the MBSR program at UMass alone. From the earliest days of MBSR, Kabat-Zinn has taught mindfulness as a secular discipline detached from any involvement with Buddhism, and he has sought to prove the practical effectiveness of mindfulness through scientific studies. Perhaps this science-based approach is a core reason for the program's popularity and the public's acceptance of mindfulness techniques.

Around the same time that Kabat-Zinn's MBSR program was gaining widespread recognition, the Dalai Lama was launching an organization—the Mind and Life Institute—whose aim was to study the convergence of mind and contemplation.[232] From its initial meeting in 1987 to the present, the Dalai Lama, the leader of Tibetan Buddhism and the head of the Tibetan government in exile, has actively participated in all of the institute's annual meetings as honorary chairman. In these gatherings, leading psychologists and neuroscientists of our time assemble to explore the relationship between science and contemplation.

The leading researcher in the field of neuroscience and mindfulness is Richard Davidson, the director of the Laboratory for Affective Neuroscience and the Center for Investigating Healthy Minds at the University of Wisconsin, Madison. He has been particularly influential in bringing scientific rigor to the study of mindfulness. Starting in 1992, with the support of the Dalai Lama, Davidson began his work with long-term Buddhist meditation practitioners.[233] Using recently developed technology—functional magnetic resonance imaging (fMRI)—Davidson began to measure, in real time, changes in the brain activity of the monks that participated in his research. To date, Davidson has examined eleven experienced mindfulness practitioners. They have each completed an estimated ten to forty thousand hours of mindfulness meditation over a span of fifteen to forty years.

Even though Christian contemplative prayer has not garnered this same attention from the scientific community, research findings indicate that we can apply findings about mindfulness to Christian contemplative prayer. David Benner, a leading Christian psychologist, points to the similarities and congruence between mindfulness and Centering Prayer.[234] Numerous secular neuroscientists and behavioral scientists support the use of Centering Prayer.[235] Neuroscientist Andrew Newberg has conducted the only scientific investigation specifically on the use and benefits of Centering Prayer, and he concludes, "The neurological effects of the Centering Prayer are nearly identical to the mindfulness practices of Buddhism." [236, 237] With strong support from the scientific community, we can confidently assume that contemplative prayer has the same neurological, psychological, and relational benefits as mindfulness.

Daniel Siegel argues that contemplative practices not only cultivate certain states of mind, but also certain personal traits.[238] As detailed in part II, Centering Prayer brings our attention back to our body. It teaches us to aim and sustain our attention. As we engage in contemplative prayer, we are training our mind to stay in the present moment. In the practice of contemplative prayer, we learn to watch the activities of our mind with acceptance. When we observe that our mind has wandered, we learn to repeatedly return our attention to God. When our mind becomes silent and the small self fades into the background, we become aware of God's presence. Freed from the ordinary functions of the mind, we find security in God's loving embrace.

The new science of contemplation is now telling us that with practice, these repeated mental states can become traits, and these traits can transform our lives. A *trait* is defined as a way of living that is present without intentional effort.[239] In other words, a trait is a quality that automatically appears in a situation without having to think about it. Research shows that a trait occurs gradually over time as a consequence of a sustained contemplative practice.

In part III, we will examine six traits that arise from regular contemplative prayer: The contemplative skill of stillness translates into the trait of *calmness.* The regular practice of letting go shows up as *attunement.* Out of openness and letting go emerges *presence.* Learning to pay attention in a special way translates into *stories of truth.* The trait of *resonance* grows out of union with God. And finally, experiencing the love of God teaches us how to be *trustworthy.*

The good news is that these six traits—cultivated through a regular practice of contemplative prayer—have the power to transform our marriage. With calmness, we learn to provide our spouse with stability. Attunement enables us to respond effectively to our spouse's emotions. With presence, we can turn toward our spouses when they are upset. Stories of truth allow us to communicate vulnerability, acceptance, and mutuality. With resonance, we can move from a position of "me" to one of "we." And finally, trustworthiness allows us to place our spouse's best interests—rather than our own—at center stage.

In part II, we examined the experience that seven clients had with Centering Prayer. They all reported that they were beginning to notice the emergence of certain traits as a result of their practice. Several related that they were becoming less reactive to their spouse's behavior. Developing a different relationship with emotions—that is, changing toward greater acceptance of their own and their partner's feelings—was a common theme. A few observed that they were "more present." Some were pleased that they were gaining some distance from their stories. As a result, they could revisit and change their original narratives. It was common to hear them report that, as a result of becoming less self-focused, they were developing greater responsiveness to their spouse's needs. All seven asked their spouses if they perceived them as more trustworthy after practicing Centering Prayer for several weeks and all of their spouses responded in the affirmative.

Nothing comes easy. The power of Centering Prayer to generate certain mental skills and associated personal traits does not happen overnight. Science is now telling us that the cultivation of these mental skills and personal traits requires a minimum of eight weeks of daily contemplative practice. Most studies report that participants experience the benefits of mindfulness when they practice forty-five minutes daily, six days a week. (Thomas Keating recommends two twenty-minute periods of prayer per day, so this is very close to the scientific standard.)

All of the clients that were described in part II engaged in a daily practice of Centering Prayer. While two clients were in the habit of praying two times a day, most were sitting once a day. Four clients followed Thomas Keating's instructions to practice for twenty minutes. The others were sitting from ten minutes to thirty minutes.

If you are ready to engage in a regular practice of Centering Prayer, the science of contemplation offers hope that this practice can not only change your mind, but change your marriage. We have turned to the Christian contemplative tradition for wisdom as we have sought to understand the nature of the mind and restore its stability. Now it is time to bring the understanding of science and Christian contemplation together as we attempt to apply the benefits of Centering Prayer to our marriage.

Try this:

1. Ask yourself: "Am I willing to commit to doing eight weeks of Centering Prayer in order to see how the practice can benefit my marriage?" If so, you will need to devote between twenty and forty minutes per day to your practice, six days a week. Remember, to see what Centering Prayer has to offer and to experience the maximum benefits, you will need to complete at least eight weeks of practice.

2. Take a self-inventory of the traits listed in this chapter. Which ones do you already possess? Are there some which you could improve? Which ones do you find most desirable? Which ones do you think could benefit your marriage most?

CHAPTER 16

Calmness

You will keep in perfect peace him whose mind
is steadfast.
—*Isaiah 26:3*

Couples who relieve distress quickly tend to be more
stable and secure.
—*Marion Solomon and Stan Tatkin,*
Love and War in Intimate Relationships

The trait of calmness refers to our ability to soothe not only our own mind, but also that of our spouse. This personal characteristic is central to marital happiness. With this attribute, we can restore stability to our mind when it gets out of balance. Calmness helps us also reconnect with our spouse after the disconnections that inevitably occur in intimate relationships. This trait enables us to restore and maintain the safety and security that we long for in our marriage.

Calming the mind starts by calming the body. In part I, we learned that anything that puts our sense of connection and security into jeopardy activates an important property of the mind: the threat response system. We also learned that once the threat system is activated, our body moves out of balance. Depending on how our mind assesses the danger, our body becomes either over-aroused or under-aroused.

If our brain assesses that we cannot do anything to protect our safety—"I am helpless"—the parasympathetic nervous system becomes activated. The heart rate falls, digestion shuts down, and sweating increases as we exhibit a freeze response. On the other hand, if our brain determines that we can handle the danger, the sympathetic nervous system is activated. Numerous physical, neurochemical, and hormonal reactions occur, which produce the energy that we need to either fight or run away.

Once the mind perceives that an interaction is not providing us with the safety and security that we desire, fear is activated. Fear quickly alters chemistries in the body, causing smooth muscles in the internal organs to contract or dilate. At the same time, the middle prefrontal cortex of the brain is being shut off. Since fear operates primarily outside of our awareness, it enlists the help of the body, memories, and perceptions to produce a protective response to the threatening situation.

Once an episode in our marriage pushes our body and mind out of balance, negative behaviors are sure to follow. Before we realize it, we are engaged in behaviors that sabotage the well-being of our marriage. As long as the body and mind are under the control of the threat response system, we will engage in behavior—attacking or withdrawing—that will create an even greater disconnection with our spouse.

When Barbara and Mike first came to see me for couple's therapy, Barbara's threat response system was on high alert. If Mike said anything that Barbara perceived as a put-down, she was quick to counter with defensiveness or an assault of her own. If she felt small, then she tried to produce a similar response in him.

Fortunately for us, the mind is equipped with a way to calm the nervous system: the soothing system.[240] A person with the trait of calmness has learned how to regulate the threat system and create physical and mental states that are conducive to a quiet mind. By soothing the mind, we are able to calm down the threat response system, turn off the fear-producing amygdala, and reduce our state of arousal.

Calming down our body has been proved to increase marital satisfaction.[241] According to one psychological study, physiological arousal almost perfectly predicts declines in marital satisfaction, while a calmer physiology predicts increases in marital satisfaction.[242] It seems that activating the physiological system blocks access to social skills such as our sense of humor, creativity, problem-solving ability, empathy, and non-defensive listening. However, these blocks are removed when our level of excitement is lowered.

So, what is the cure for having a body that is out of balance? How do we calm it down? The first cure is self-soothing. There are several methods that we can utilize for self-soothing (or self-regulating). The first skill is monitoring the body.[243] During times when the body is highly aroused, we scan our body for tension and practice letting it go. Diaphragmatic breathing can be useful to let off any bodily tension. Taking a break of at least twenty minutes is very important for some people.

Self-regulating is useful for some spouses, but not others.[244] The key seems to be our attachment style. In chapter 5, we learned that some people employ an anxious style, reaching out to others to regulate their arousal, while others who are more apt to turn inward use an avoidant style when they are physiologically aroused. The avoidant spouse may find self-regulating useful, whereas the anxious spouse may become even more out of balance if they have to deal with the arousal alone.

Barbara acknowledged that her practice of Centering Prayer was leading her toward an avoidant style. Therefore, recently when she got upset with Mike, her preference was to first turn inward. Doing this allowed her to contain her reaction, observe her physical sensations, and make room for the emotion. However, within a relatively short period of time, she did want to talk to Mike about the situation, if he was open to conversing.

Increasingly, marriage counselors are encouraging us to utilize another cure for calming down our body: co-regulation (or mutual regulation).[245] With co-regulation, we discard the do-it-yourself mentality and embrace an attitude of taking care of each other. Many of us have been taught that we should be responsible for ourselves and not expect someone else to look after us. Mutual regulation, on the other hand, actually encourages us to improve our ability to calm down and care for our spouse.

If our job is to relieve our spouse of stress, it is important for us to develop useful skills. The first skill is learning how to read one another's arousal. In other words, we must notice and respond to bodily cues that our spouse is in a state of excitement. Perhaps the distress is communicated in their posture, tone of voice, or facial expression. We must develop an internal manual of how our spouse communicates high states of arousal.

Physical comfort seems to be a key method for co-regulating a spouse who is distressed. Research reveals that comfort calms down the threat response system. In one study, it was discovered that when a woman is happily married and her husband is holding her hand, almost all physiological arousal disappears, even in the presence of alarm and danger signals.[246] In another study, the researcher developed a method—having partners sit close to each other with thighs touching—for helping couples create warm support.[247] For couples who were satisfied with their relationship, both the men and women secreted oxytocin during this experience. Oxytocin decreased noradrenaline levels and blood pressure rates for the women in this study.

Several studies show that oxytocin has the power to induce calmness and contentment. How can these effects by explained? In one study, when oxytocin was spritzed into the noses of the participants—which allowed it to go directly to their brains—it reduced activation of the amygdala.[248] This study suggests that oxytocin can quiet the amygdala and thus induce feelings of calmness.

Research by John Gottman reveals that a wife's trust of her husband can also have a soothing effect. How much she trusts him is what matters physiologically to both spouses. In other words, if the wife trusts her husband, the blood pressure levels for both partners goes down.

For some undiscovered reason, the husband's trust of his wife does not have similar effects on their blood pressure.

The last skill that helps soothe an excited nervous system is the human voice.[249] How we use our voice has a powerful impact on calming our spouse. Have you noticed how your volume, tone, rate of speech, and pitch affects your spouse's level of arousal? Begin paying attention to—and taking notes on—how your voice can soothe your spouse when he or she is distressed.

What is the connection between calmness and contemplative practices? Most of the research that examines the relationship between calmness and contemplation focuses on mindfulness. The first truly randomized controlled trial of mindfulness-based stress reduction (MBSR) was conducted in 1999.[250] The first thing the research showed was that anxiety symptoms fell by about 12 percent among the people who took the eight-week class but increased slightly among the wait-list control group. The researchers concluded that MBSR, by helping people better cope with stress, speeded up recovery from emotional upsets.

Only one study has closely examined the impact that MBSR has on couples.[251] The couples participating in this study practiced mindfulness for an average of thirty-two minutes per day over an eight-week period. The results showed that mindfulness brought about significant improvements in day-to-day relationship stress and overall stress. Greater mindfulness practice on a given day was associated, on that same day and for several consecutive days, with improved levels of overall stress.

Scientific research informs us that Centering Prayer has the same calming effects as mindfulness, but how does Centering Prayer quiet the body and mind? There are four main reasons. First, when Centering Prayer becomes part of our daily lives through the Welcoming Prayer, we learn to pay better attention to our body. Step one in the Welcoming Prayer—focus and sink in—teaches us to focus our attention on physical sensations and experience them. Learning to read our own physiological signs prepares us to read our spouse's physical signs of arousal. In order to soothe the stress in our own and our spouse's bodies, we must first recognize the physical signs of its presence.

As a result of her practice in Centering Prayer and Welcoming Prayer, Barbara had developed a greater awareness of the physical sensations that accompanied her painful feelings. For example, she could tell if her blood pressure went up, if she was clenching her jaw, or if her stomach was in a knot. She said, "I try to notice and make room for the tension," meaning she tried to sit with and accept the physical sensations. Paradoxically, by accepting the tension, she was actually able to let go of the stress more quickly.

Once we have welcomed the physical sensations associated with stressful emotions, we must master the art of letting go of the physical sensations and tension. (You will remember from chapter 12 that Centering Prayer boils down to one exercise: letting go.) The practice of letting go is not a practice of pushing away, judging, or rejecting painful emotions and the physical sensations that accompany them. Instead, letting go, as it is practiced in the Welcoming Prayer, is more of a "being with." The Welcoming Prayer, as it is practiced amidst the stressful events of our daily life, teaches us to sit with our own—and our spouse's—intense feelings and aroused bodies. The emotions and physical sensations are not pushed away prematurely. Instead, they are allowed to dissolve on their own accord as we notice and accept them.

A third way that Centering Prayer helps us quiet our body and mind is through its emphasis on breathing. Basil Pennington teaches us to use three deep breaths as preparation for Centering Prayer. Thomas Keating encourages us to use our breath as a sacred word if a word does not help us let go of the thoughts, emotions, and physical sensations that arise during Centering Prayer. Scientific research shows that deep breathing is useful in letting go of physical tension.

Finally, Centering Prayer, with its emphasis on union, prepares us to engage in co-regulating our spouse's tension. The contemplative experience of union reveals that the separation that we sense with God and others is just a grand illusion generated by the mind. Through unitive experiences, the wall of separation comes down and we realize an amazing connection. We realize that our minds and bodies are somehow intertwined. If our spouse is in distress, love leads us to provide the comfort that brings quiet to their mind and body.

Barbara discovered the connection between calming herself and Mike. She put it this way: "When my body is filled with tension, I try to notice it and let it be there. That is my way of letting it go. When I stay open to myself, a natural caring emerges. Caring for myself quickly moves to caring for Mike. After listening to my own body for a while, I am more prepared to listen to Mike. I actually want to listen to and care for him. It is now not just about how I feel. It is about how both of us feel."

Now that we have examined the relationship between calmness and contemplative practices, what is the connection between calmness, contemplative practices, and neurobiology? First, what is going on in the brains of people who have trouble restoring calmness after they are filled with tension? Richard Davidson points out that people who have trouble regaining their physical and mental balance have fewer signals traveling from the prefrontal cortex to the amygdala. This can arise from low activity in the left prefrontal cortex itself or from the lack of connections between the left prefrontal cortex and the amygdala.[252]

Davidson goes on to describe how mindfulness changes the brain. His research shows that participants in MBSR classes show greater activation in circuits in the left prefrontal cortex and stronger connections between the left prefrontal cortex and the amygdala. These changes in functions of the brain seem to be responsible for quickly restoring balance to the body and mind after an upsetting event.

How do these changes help people bounce back from upsetting events? According to Davidson, activation of the left prefrontal cortex inhibits the amygdala. Strong neuronal connections between the left prefrontal cortex and the amygdala enable the prefrontal cortex to send signals to the excited amygdala to quiet down. By inhibiting the amygdala, the prefrontal cortex helps us bounce back quickly from a threatening situation.

Scientific research assures us that a regular practice of Centering Prayer restores mental balance after a time of stress. By altering brain structures and functions, Centering Prayer helps us establish the trait of calmness. By responding effectively to the physical and emotional signs of distress, the quality of calmness assists us in establishing a stable and satisfying marriage. I was taken aback one day during a session with Barbara and Mike when she ended the conversation with these words, "I am more interested in doing things the calm way versus the right way."

Try this:

1. Notice your reactions to your spouse this week. Be aware when you respond from the threat response system. How does this system affect your spouse? Observe when your response comes from the soothing system. How does your spouse respond to this system?

2. Do a self-evaluation regarding your ability to calm yourself down.
   a) How well do you notice the physical signals that you are stressed?
   b) How do you react to these physical sensations? Do you allow them to be present, or do you try to push them away?
   c) Do you use deep breathing to bring relaxation to your body and mind?

3. Do an assessment in terms of co-regulating:
   a) Do you reach out to your spouse when you are upset?
   b) Does your spouse reach out to you when he or she is stressed?
   c) How skilled are you when it comes to reading your spouse's emotional and physical arousal?

d) Is your spouse skilled in terms of reading your arousal?

e) Is physical touch soothing for you? What type of touch?

f) Is physical touch soothing for your spouse? What type of touch?

g) Does your voice have a calming effect on your spouse?

h) Does your spouse's voice have a calming effect on you?

i) Sit close to your spouse with thighs touching. Does it have a calming effect on you? On your spouse?

j) If you are the husband, rate how much you think your wife trusts you. (1 is very low while 10 is very high.) If you are the wife, rate how much you trust your husband. (Use the same rating scale.) Looking at your blood pressure, do you agree or disagree with Gottman's conclusion that the wife's trust in her husband affects the blood pressure of both partners?

CHAPTER 17

Attunement

When Jesus saw her crying . . . he was deeply disturbed and troubled.

—John 11:33

Attunement is how we focus our attention on others and take their essence into our inner world.

—Daniel Siegel, The Mindful Therapist

Do you remember the last time your spouse was overwhelmed with feelings of sadness, fear, or anger? How did you respond? Did you wind up feeling like you had done or said the wrong thing? Did you come away feeling totally incompetent when it came to dealing effectively with your spouse's negative emotions? If so, you were lacking attunement in that emotional situation. In this chapter, we will find out about attunement. What is it? What does it look like? How is it related to a regular Centering Prayer practice?

Attunement is defined as the trait of responding effectively to your spouse's emotions. According to science, when we respond effectively to our spouse's emotions, three important things happen. First, attunement generates a sense of security.[253] We know that feeling close and connected to our spouse determines the stability of our marriage. When our spouse feels insecure, his or her threat response is activated, resulting in a cascade of negative mental events and destructive behaviors. Second, when we respond effectively to our spouse's emotions, it has a calming effect on their mind.[254] As a result of attunement, our spouse's threat response system begins to quiet down, their physiological arousal begins to subside, and their mind comes back into balance. Finally, attunement is a major mechanism through which couples build trust, the sense that our spouse is there for us.[255] With attunement, we are showing our spouse that we are there for them when they are overwhelmed with negative emotions.

Research reveals that many of our marital problems are rooted in our philosophy about emotions.[256] Should emotions be experienced? Is it a good thing to explore them? Is it best to express them? If your answer to all of these questions was no, then we would say that you have a dismissing philosophy. This kind of attitude toward emotions communicates several things. First, it sends the message that we don't want to hear about our spouse's feelings. Second, emotion-dismissing suggests that our spouse could—and should—change their emotion: "If you wanted to, you could change how you are feeling. You just aren't trying hard enough." Finally, a person with a dismissing attitude is probably taking personal responsibility for making their spouse feel better. Unfortunately, we cannot make our spouse feel a certain way.

During the early part of my work with Ron and Natalie, Ron had a dismissing attitude. He didn't realize it, but during our first couple sessions, he usually turned his body away from Natalie when she began to express strong emotions. He eventually disclosed that he felt overwhelmed by her intense feelings, so he was just trying to calm himself down. Ron's bottom line was that Natalie was too emotional and that she should talk with a calmer tone of voice. If she did get upset, Ron felt responsible for fixing it somehow. He felt helpless in his inability to prevent her from getting upset and then calming her down once she became agitated.

What are we to do? Psychologist John Gottman suggests shifting our philosophy from dismissing to attunement.[257] This shift means giving up responsibility for changing our spouse's emotions. When our spouse is upset, we are there to pay attention, understand, listen, empathize, and accept—not change him or her.

Gottman uses the acronym ATTUNE to capture the characteristics of attunement:

Awareness of the emotion,
Turning toward the emotion,
Tolerance of the emotional experience,
Understanding of the emotion,
Non-defensive listening to the emotion, and
Empathy toward the emotion.

The first characteristic of attunement is *attention*. Attention refers to how we focus on the emotional signals being sent by our spouse. Research from neuroscience reveals that negative emotions generated in the right amygdala generally act outside of our awareness and are expressed through body language. Since we are on the outside—paying attention to our spouse—we can be on the lookout for emotional signals that their body is sending. With attention, we are observing our spouse's eyes, tone of voice, posture, and facial expressions. All of these nonverbal signals send messages about what our spouse is feeling on the inside.

Perhaps Jesus was speaking about attention when he said, "Don't you have eyes? Why can't you see? Don't you have ears? Why can't you hear?" (Mark 8:18) We usually attribute spiritual meaning to this passage, but I think it can be applied in a very practical way to our marital relationship. Sitting right beside our spouse, don't we sometimes fail to see the strained expression on their face or hear the distressed sound in their voice? It is as if we don't have eyes and ears. However, the trait of attunement awakens our senses—opens our eyes and ears—so that we can see that look of fear and hear that sound of pain.

The first *T* in ATTUNE is for *turning toward*. Turning toward requires a mental shift from thinking that something is wrong with our spouse for having a negative emotion. There can be no blaming or fault-finding with this second attribute of attunement. Instead, we genuinely want to know what our spouse is feeling. We realize that behind a strong emotion is a need or desire. Ask yourself, "Beneath this emotion, what does my spouse want? What does my spouse need from me in this situation?"

The second *T* in ATTUNE stands for *tolerance.* Tolerance is recognition of our spouse's perception of an event or situation. Even though we may not agree when our spouse says, for example, "You are not listening to me," we still treat their perception of the interaction and their feelings as important. We may not adopt this perspective as our own, but we avoid arguing about the facts and are tolerant of their perspective. For example, when your spouse accuses you of not listening, you may know that you were in fact listening to your spouse, but you remain open to conversing about their experience of the event.

The fourth characteristic of attunement is *understanding.* Understanding refers to our desire to discover the meaning of our spouse's emotion. How do they make sense out of the event that triggered their negative emotion? Is there some history behind how they responded to the situation? Of course, with understanding, we must focus on our spouse's point of view and postpone our own agenda. When we are trying to understand our spouse, it is not the right time to persuade them to see the situation from our perspective.

The *N* in ATTUNE stands for *non-defensive listening.* This is probably the most difficult skill in attunement. It involves recognizing our own negative emotions and working to stay calm. When our spouse gets upset with us and accuses us of doing something offensive—"You were being selfish and inconsiderate"—our initial reaction may be to get angry and argue. However, with non-defensive listening, we remind ourselves of something important: "My spouse has a right to her perception of the event. We are not discussing facts, even though my spouse may be sounding as though we are. Remember to breathe, keep quiet, and listen."

The final letter in ATTUNE stands for *empathy*. Empathy is the skill of understanding what your spouse feels, and communicating that understanding. It captures all five sub-skills in the other letters of ATTUNE. Empathy refers to paying attention to our spouse's nonverbal emotional signals. We genuinely want to understand how they feel. It is about seeing the situation through their eyes. And finally, empathy enables us to stay in a position of listening. As a result, we might respond with this message: "It makes sense that you are upset because you thought that I wasn't listening. You really need for me to take you seriously."

Let's now turn our attention to the question of how attunement—the trait of effectively responding to the emotions of our spouse—is related to the practice of Centering Prayer. First, attention is clearly a mental skill that we cultivate through the practice of contemplation. In chapter 10, we learned that attention is the narrowing of our focus to our intention. Our intention is the thing upon which we decide to focus. In attunement, our intention is the emotion of our spouse. Whenever we become aware that our attention has wandered to another focus—say for example, our own perspective—we remember to return our attention to our spouse's emotions and perspective of the situation.

Before Ron began his practice of Centering Prayer, it was nearly impossible for him to pay attention when Natalie became emotional. He thought that he must somehow fix her feelings, and his automatic reaction was to turn away and stop listening. Once he learned—through the Welcoming Prayer—to welcome his own emotions, he became more skilled at allowing and accepting her feelings. When it dawned on him that he didn't have to resolve or judge her feelings, he was able to just listen as Natalie expressed her feelings of pain.

What is the neurobiology of attention? How can contemplation change the brain so that we become more skilled at reading our spouse's body language and picking up on nonverbal cues? Again, Richard Davidson provides us with answers to these questions.[258] His research reveals that a deficiency in attention comes from high levels of activation in the amygdala and low levels of activation in the fusiform. (The fusiform is located on the underside of the temporal lobe of the cortex and it is important in the processing of vision and faces.) To improve our attention to vocal and facial cues, we need to pump up fusiform activity and quiet down amygdala activity.

Davidson offers two suggestions for accomplishing these two goals.[259] To increase neuronal activity in the fusiform, he instructs us to engage in training that will improve our ability to detect nonverbal signals. This training involves specific exercises that cause us to focus on other people's tone of voice, facial expressions, and body language. (We will examine a modified version of this exercise at the end of this chapter.)

To quiet amygdala activity—which will help with improving our ability to read body language—Davidson recommends the practice of mindfulness. We learned in chapter 16 that practitioners of mindfulness show greater activation in the left prefrontal cortex and stronger connections between the left prefrontal cortex and the amygdala. These changes to the functions of the brain enable the prefrontal cortex to effectively send signals to the amygdala to quiet down.

What is the connection between *turning toward*—the second skill in attunement—and Centering Prayer? In order to address this question, we must first identify the difference between the left and right prefrontal regions of the cortex. Neuroscience informs us that the left prefrontal region appears to be associated with an approach state, whereas right prefrontal activation is associated with withdrawal.[260] In order to turn toward, or approach, our spouse's negative emotions, we must reduce energy levels in the right side and raise activity in the left side. This is where a contemplative practice is effective, because research shows that mindfulness and Centering Prayer increase activity in the left prefrontal cortex. This shift from right to left moves us toward more of an approach mentality.

There is a direct connection between contemplation and the attunement skills of tolerance, understanding, and non-defensive listening. In chapter 12, we learned that Centering Prayer boils down to one exercise: letting go. In Centering Prayer, we are continually releasing our thoughts. We attempt to adhere to the Four Rs: resist no thought, retain no thought, react to no thought, and return to the sacred word. By not giving emotions, memories, and narratives our attention—by emptying our mind—we are ultimately letting go of the small self. You will recall that the small self possesses a sense of knowing and it likes to be at the center. The practice of contemplation is an exercise in removing the self from its central role.

Over time, the Centering Prayer practice of letting go produces the trait of attunement. We display tolerance when we set aside our own perception of an event to recognize our spouse's perception of the situation. By postponing our own agenda and focusing on our spouse's perception, we exhibit the skill of understanding. And finally, by resisting the urge to defend our self—that is, to be right—and to put our self at the center, we are able to engage in non-defensive listening.

When I first started working with Ron and Natalie, Ron was defensive. If Natalie said something that Ron perceived as criticism, he was quick to give her evidence that what she said wasn't true. He went to great lengths to explain himself, thinking that he could shape her view so that she eventually agreed with him. He wanted her to see him as a good person. It seemed to him that the most important thing was for her to be happy with him.

After regularly practicing Centering Prayer and the Welcoming Prayer for several weeks, Ron's response to Natalie had shifted. He began to make room for Natalie's emotions; he began to just listen. If she was upset with him, it did not bother him as much as it used to. Perhaps he was beginning to find some internal security. It was okay if Natalie didn't see him as a good person at that exact moment in time. He knew on the inside that he was a good person. And besides, she didn't have to always be happy with him. In addition, he began to value Natalie's emotional side.

Numerous scientific studies reveal that a contemplative practice offers a unique means of cultivating empathy. One randomized controlled trial examined the effects of an eight-week MBSR intervention for medical and premedical students.[261] Findings indicated significant increases in empathy levels in medical students as compared to the control group. Another study examining the effects of MBSR on counseling psychology students also found significant increases in empathy.[262]

Science is interested in how contemplation increases our capacity for empathy. One theory is that a regular contemplative practice—such as mindfulness or Centering Prayer—reduces stress, and that a reduction in stress is associated with an increase in empathy.[263] In chapter 16, we discussed the findings of studies that demonstrated that participants of MBSR experienced significant drops in their stress levels. Other studies show that by simply reducing our stress we can cultivate greater empathy. The second theory is that contemplation helps us cultivate empathy by helping us dis-identify with our own perspective.

When we are not caught up in ourselves, we have room to attend to our spouse. By shifting our perspective beyond our own personal, subjective experience we gain an increased ability to entertain the perspective of our spouse. Ron was learning not only to entertain Natalie's approach to life, but also to value it. One day during a session, Ron put it this way: "Natalie goes with an emotional response before going with a thinking response. I tend to do just the opposite. Now, I am less apt to judge her for her style. I just accept that this is how she deals with life, and I'm actually beginning to appreciate and applaud her for being emotional."

Try this:

1. Notice this week when you deal effectively with your spouse's emotions. How does it affect him or her?

2. Observe a time this week when you respond ineffectively to your spouse's emotions. Don't judge yourself for this. Just be aware of it.

3. *Evaluate your response to your spouse's emotions. Do you have a dismissing or attuned philosophy? Do you think you have to change your spouse's emotions? Do you think it is enough to simply pay attention, understand, listen, and empathize?*

4. *Assess how attuned you are to your spouse's emotions.*
   a) Do you notice the emotional signals that your spouse's body is sending?
   b) Do you judge your spouse for having certain emotions?
   c) Do you make space for your spouse's perspective?
   d) Can you postpone your own point of view long enough to understand your spouse's perspective?
   e) Do you listen non-defensively?
   f) Do you communicate that you understand what your spouse is feeling?

5. *Try this exercise to improve your attention to vocal and social cues.*[264] *When your spouse is talking to someone else on the phone, in a social situation, or in a professional setting, watch him or her closely. Pay particular attention to your spouse's face. Does your spouse's tone of voice match their body language and facial expression?*

CHAPTER 18

Presence

You will fill me with joy in your presence.
—Psalm 16:11

Humans deeply desire presence. That is why we are
so vulnerable to absence.
—David Benner, Soulful Spirituality

Do you remember the last time you were sitting right beside your spouse and he or she asked, "Where are you?" It seemed like such a silly question, so you replied with some indignation, "I'm right here!" But your partner wasn't asking about the location of your body; of course your physical being was there. But you were probably lost in thought. Maybe you were distracted by a memory from either the distant or recent past. Perhaps you had moved ahead into the future, thinking about some upcoming event. Or possibly, you were captured by an emotional experience. Your spouse did not know where your mind had taken you. He or she only knew that you were absent.

In this chapter we will explore the trait of *presence,* which we will define as being fully present. It is harder than it sounds. What are the qualities of being present? How do we develop it? What is the neurobiology of presence? And how is it related to Centering Prayer?

Daniel Siegel identifies openness as one of the core qualities of presence.[265] Let's examine this word, openness. It is the opposite of closed. When something is closed, let's say, a door, nothing can come in or go out. There is a separation between that which is on the outside and that which is on the inside. But openness suggests that the barrier has come down. With presence, energy and information flow freely between spouses.

Openness can also be described as receptivity. This means that we are in a stance of receiving. Think about your posture when you are receiving a gift. Your hands are open and you take in what the other person gives. Isn't this what we do when we are open with our spouse? We accept what they give us as a gift and we respond with kindness and compassion.

The opposite of being receptive is being reactive. When we react to our spouse, we turn away from the experience that is happening between our partner and us. Because of some activity in our mind—a judgment, an uncomfortable emotion, an unconscious memory, our own perspective—we tighten our hands and bodies as we withdraw from the interaction. Our mind is saying, "No, I can't be present to you right now with love and kindness." Daniel Siegel writes, "When we are reactive, presence is shut off."[266]

When Linda and Steve showed up at my office, Linda was quick to react in anger to interactions that she perceived as negative. Her first instinct was to control the situation. Perhaps she would use persuasion in an attempt to get Steve to change his behavior. If that didn't work, then she might resort to personal attacks so that things would turn out the way that she intended. Her behavior was the opposite of loving and kind.

When does openness takes place? The answer is "Now, in this present moment." Presence doesn't occur yesterday or tomorrow but right now. But it is hard to stay in the present. Our mind seems to be almost hardwired to be pulled into the past and pushed into the future, while it avoids the present. Neuroscience tells us that as we interact with our spouse in the present, this information enters the amygdala, which is home to our deepest implicit memories. In a split second, our mind is lost in a memory or emotion, and these unconscious memories shade our perceptions and emotional responses to the present experience. Our mind also likes to dream of the future, planning for some upcoming event. But the mind is not so comfortable with the present, here and now. No wonder presence is so difficult to come by.

Now, we are beginning to touch on the barriers to being present with our spouse. What can we do about it? First, we can live more fully in the present when we allow our implicit memories to become explicit.[267] Daniel Siegel teaches us to do this by identifying intense physical and emotional reactions to a particular event. This is the first sign of an implicit memory. Once we have identified an event that provokes a particularly strong emotional reaction, we must sit with that feeling and entertain the possibility that it may be connected with a past event that is outside of our awareness. As we examine this possibility, the link that memory makes between the past and present may become clearer.

After several weeks of practicing Centering Prayer and the Welcoming Prayer, Linda was beginning to notice her physical reactions to Steve's behavior. Her most common response was a tightening in her stomach. She interpreted this tension as a sign of reactivity. In the past, she would have immediately launched into action to change the situation more to her liking. But now, instead of responding instantly to the undesired event, she was learning to sit with the tension.

The second major barrier to being present with our spouse is reacting in judgment. Jon Kabat-Zinn, the founder of MBSR, observes, "When you begin paying attention to what's on your mind, you rapidly discover that basically everything is a judgment of one kind or another."[268] We have trouble receiving what our spouse offers us because we have opinions about almost everything. Instead of being present to an experience with our spouse, we judge: "I can't believe you are saying that! You are wrong. You don't remember it the way it happened. I don't see it that way. That is so crazy!" How can we be open to our spouse when we have all these judgments blocking our ability to be present?

This is where a second quality of presence becomes vitally important: acceptance.[269] Acceptance is about receiving things as they are at
this moment. Acceptance is about non-judgment. Acceptance says, "I
don't have to change, remove, or judge what my spouse is offering me
right now." Acceptance is not about passive resignation, about being
a doormat, or about being walked over.[270] Instead, it is about seeing
things as they are right now. Acceptance frees us from the narrative
in our heads that says things have to be a certain way at this present
moment. No, things are the way they are. My spouse is feeling a certain
way right now, even if I find it unpleasant. I can be in this moment
without it having to be different. Acceptance asks, "Can I see things the
way they are right now?" The ability to see clearly in this moment may
help us act with love and wisdom in the next moment.

Linda shared a story that reflected her increased ability to be accepting: "Just yesterday, when Steve and the kids came into the house, they
were yelling and being rambunctious. They were laughing and slam-
ming doors. In the past, I would have reacted angrily, thinking that
they should be more thoughtful as they entered the house. I would
have said something to let them know that they needed to calm down.
However, on this occasion, instead of reacting, I felt a tightness in my
stomach. I sat with the tension, resisting the impulse to do something
that would change the situation to my liking." Through this story,
Linda has shown her growing acceptance of her circumstances—she is
becoming more present.

The third quality of presence is curiosity.[271] Curiosity acts in tandem
with acceptance to pay attention to what is. Doesn't it radically alter
our view of our spouse when we start paying attention to how they
are instead of comparing them to some external standard? Haven't we
really stopped paying attention to our spouse when we think that we
know them or have them figured out? Presence resists this tendency
to become too familiar with our spouse. In this moment, we have the
opportunity to discover something new and mysterious about the other
person. When asked about his thirty-year relationship with his wife,

Gabriel García Márquez, the great Columbian novelist, responded, "I know her so well now that I have not the slightest idea who she really is."[272] Clearly, he continued to stay curious about and present to his wife.

According to Diane Gehart and Eric McCollum, two prominent marriage counselors, presence is a way of being.[273] What is this way of being? First, it is about being open to all parts of our spouse's experience. It is about accepting their thoughts, emotions, and point of view at this moment in time. Next, presence is about being open to the different facets of our own experience. What physical sensations, memories, emotions, images, and beliefs are being triggered in you at this particular moment? Can you be open to, curious about, and accepting of them? Finally, presence is about being able to respond to the immediacy of this moment. Are you able to respond with wisdom and love to the situation that is happening right now? If so, then you are manifesting presence.

By now, you know that presence does not come easily. There are many obstacles to this way of being. We have already examined the challenges posed by implicit memories and judgment. We will now uncover another obstacle: our self. David Benner, a Christian psychologist, says that we are often too full of ourselves to be available to others.[274] We think we know what to do. But we are boxed in by our opinions, preconceptions, and perceptions. We are dominated by our own feelings and beliefs about how things should operate. We have already decided how things must be. What is the answer? In order to be fully present to our spouse, we must find freedom from these mental activities. Benner writes, "Emptying must precede any genuine presence."[275]

Let's now turn our attention to a question that was posed at the beginning of the chapter: how is presence related to a contemplative practice? David Benner tells us that presence is "born out of stillness and nurtured by silence."[276] This is clearly a call to contemplative prayer.

In chapter 11, we learned that Centering Prayer involves watching a long line of mental visitors. At the front of the line may be a disturbing memory, next is an unpleasant emotion, and finally, some rambling commentary shows up. In contemplative prayer, we watch with curiosity as each thought shows up. We don't resist the thought, nor do we react to it. We simply keep releasing each thought as it appears on the screen of our mind.

Contemplative prayer orients our mind to the present moment. And if the object of our attention is anything other than God, we use the sacred word to bring us back to our original intention.

We continue to exercise acceptance during our regular practice of Centering Prayer. Time after time, we bring our attention back to our intention without judgment. We learn to refrain from judging thoughts that enter our mind during our time of prayer, because this would violate one of the four Rs: react to no thought. In addition, we abstain from the habit of judging ourselves for having the thought. Instead, when a thought shows up in our mind, we simply use our sacred word to release the thought and then shift our attention back to our original intention.

In chapter 12, we learned that the core skill of Centering Prayer is letting go. By releasing our thoughts in contemplative prayer, we are relieving the self of its duties. It seems as if we are being emptied of self or as if the self is dying. Instead of encouraging the small self to fulfill its roles of knowing, narrating, and judging, we are making room for a deeper region of the mind.

A regular practice of Centering Prayer allows us to repeatedly practice the skills of openness and letting go. On a daily basis, we are exercising muscles of attention, openness, present-mindedness, and acceptance. Over time, we are liberated from our mental prison, a prison run by fear and self. With time, we learn to forget about ourselves—and this is where love begins. As John O'Donohue writes, "Love begins . . . with an act of gracious self-forgetting."[277] Freed from the shackles of our ordinary mind, we can now turn to God for love and security. Now, we can approach life from a different stance, a position of presence.

Linda was learning how to forget about her self. She told this story:

"Steve and I were out with some friends the other day, and I thought that Steve was getting all the attention. I was able to catch that familiar sense of tightness in my stomach, and I noticed the thought that accompanied it: 'I'm not getting much recognition.' As soon as I thought that I kind of laughed to myself and said, 'Here we go again.' You can tell that this is a recurring theme for me. Anyway, observing it and accepting it helped me let it go. I was able to forget about myself and have a good time."

Turning to science, we find evidence that contemplative practices help us cultivate the trait of presence. In the previous chapter, we discovered from neuroscience that the left prefrontal cortex appears to be associated with an approach state, whereas right prefrontal activation is linked with a withdrawal state.[278] Since contemplation increases activity in the left prefrontal cortex, this shift from right to left moves us from reactivity to receptivity. Receptivity is at the heart of presence.

Richard Davidson gives us insight into the neurobiology of openness and acceptance, both essential components of presence.[279] His studies reveal that these mental qualities are associated with enhanced activation in the brain of the prefrontal cortex and the parietal cortex. And how can one increase activity in these areas of the brain? You guessed it. Through a contemplative practice. Davidson's work with practitioners of mindfulness—whose results are similar to those of Centering Prayer—revealed that their practice increased activation in the prefrontal and parietal cortices.

Davidson's research shows that contemplation, by increasing our capacity for openness and acceptance, increases our capacity for presence. His studies show that with a regular practice of contemplation people have improved their ability to tune in to themselves and others. They have become increasingly skilled at paying attention to the signals coming from their own bodies, their thoughts, and their feelings, as well as cues from others. And as they increase their awareness, they also become less judgmental. These behaviors are at the heart of presence.

In the last chapter of the Gospel of Luke, Luke tells a wonderful story of Jesus traveling with two disciples to Emmaus. Walking for hours, Jesus enters into dialogue with them and eventually shares dinner with them at the end of the day. After the dinner, the two disciples say to each other, "Weren't our hearts on fire when he spoke to us along the road?" (Luke 24:32). I think the fire that the disciples felt in their hearts was the presence of love, don't you?

When we are truly present, as Jesus was with these disciples, all barriers come down and there is a powerful flow of energy between us and our spouse. With presence, we feel love. Don't we all long to experience the warmth caused by the flame of presence?

Try this:

1. Several times this week, as you are sitting with your spouse, bring yourself into the present moment by saying to yourself, "I am sitting beside my spouse."

2. Notice your unique physical sensations that accompany reactivity. When something is not going the way you would like, ask yourself, "How is my body reacting?" Remember, don't judge yourself for reacting. Just observe your physical response.

3. Be aware of how you react to your spouse. Ask yourself, "What is my spouse doing that I don't like? How do I want things to be?" Then, see if you can receive the situation as it is at that moment. See if you can put aside any judgment—for a moment—of things as they are.

4. Pay special attention to one thing that your spouse is saying or doing today. Ask yourself these three questions: "What is he/she thinking right now? What is she/he feeling right now? What is his/her point of view regarding this event?"

CHAPTER 19

Stories of Truth

*The story-of-us about our partner and our relationship
turns out to become an index of what will eventually
happen to the relationship.*
— John Gottman, *The Science of Trust*

The truth will set you free.

— John 8:32

Has your spouse ever accused you of "telling a story"? What they probably meant was that you were telling a lie. How do we move from stories that are perceived as fabrications to stories that ring of truth? In this chapter, we will be examining the trait of telling the truth. This trait is at the heart of our marriage, and it will probably determine whether our marriage succeeds or fails. Without this quality, we will be imprisoned in narratives that are negative, self-protective, and self-serving. It is only by telling stories of truth that we have the hope of being free, free to experience a satisfying, secure, and healthy marriage.

We are all storytellers! We cannot help but create stories about our partner, our marriage, and ourselves. Our mind is motivated to come up with explanations for the interactions that happen between our spouse and ourselves. However, in its drive and hurry, it often overlooks an important detail—the stories are actually more fiction than fact. Our internal dialogue feels like truth to us, but it is usually far from being objectively true. How does this happen? How can we remedy this situation?

In the beginning of my work with David and Rachel, Rachel had two dominant stories about David. Her first was that he had a tendency to withdraw when he got upset. Her second was that he left her with the primary burden of parenting while he pursued his career as a landscape designer. Both of these stories placed the blame on David for their marital woes.

What are the important elements of stories that are missing the ring of truth? First, an event triggers our threat response system, which activates our self-protection mechanism. As soon as the threat response system is activated, raw material from our right brain—memories and emotions—begins to take shape in the form of a story. Outside of our awareness, our mind begins to create a personal story that provides us with an explanation of what happened. In an attempt to protect ourselves, the cause is typically identified as our spouse. We begin to construct a negative story that places our spouse at fault for the unhappy event.

Let's take a more detailed look at each of these elements of an "untruthful" narrative, beginning with self-protection. We have learned how quickly the threat response system becomes activated when our sense of security is threatened. When our spouse does or fails to do something that makes us feel unloved, unwanted, and unappreciated, we immediately feel threatened. Then, our immediate response is to move into a self-protective position. All of our responses that follow—including our narratives—serve the purpose of protecting us from further danger. Telling stories is our fundamental tactic of self-protection.

In its rush to construct a self-protective story, our mind operates independently. There may be many views of the situation, but because we are on alert we are not able to step outside ourselves to view our spouse, our marriage, and ourselves in an impartial fashion. As a result, we can only see things from one viewpoint: our own.

Viewing the event from only one angle—our own—creates two significant problems for the integrity of the story. First, the story becomes selective. In other words, only certain information is picked to make its way into the story. Since we do not recognize this property of the mind, we tend to think that our stories are accurate and complete. Unbeknownst to us, the events that don't fit our typical story typically get cut. We become unreliable narrators.

Second, the story provides a cause or explanation of the event. Now we are responding to the question: who caused the problem, and why? Since we are the narrator of our own tale, we decide that the difficulty probably resulted from something our spouse did. We are the hero and our spouse is the villain. They, because of a flaw or shortcoming, are at fault and to blame.

Because stories are interested in the aims or intentions of other people, we will typically wonder: why is he doing this? When we attribute malevolent purposes to our spouse—as our story so often does—we turn them into the enemy or a stranger. When this happens, the story takes a negative turn. As John Gottman observes, when the story becomes negative, the relationship begins to follow a sad, predictable trajectory.[280]

In order to tell stories of truth, we must make several crucial changes. First, we must gain some distance from narratives by viewing them in a historical context. Second, we must tell stories that include our own vulnerabilities. This may require bringing unconscious material into awareness. Third, we must develop accounts that focus on descriptions rather than explanations. Next, we must work on telling stories-of-us. And finally, we must turn our narratives in a positive direction.

How do we gain distance from our narratives? Andrew Christensen and Neil Jacobson, developers of Integrative Behavioral Couple Therapy, suggest that the most effective way to gain distance from stories is to view them in a historical context.[281] This means that we look at a current event in terms of how we were raised and the role that we played in our family of origin. Looking at the interaction from this vantage point enables us to move from blame and fault-finding to one of understanding and acceptance. Instead of seeing our spouse as bad or wrong, we simply see them as a product of their personal history.

Our stories take a helpful turn when we shift from self-protection and blame to a focus on vulnerabilities.[282] Now, our story is not so much about the offending action but about how early experiences in our life triggered our response to the action. This story will focus less on our spouse's actions and more on our own thoughts, memories, and emotions that arose in response to the provocative action. We are not justifying our response, supporting it with a rational argument, or presenting it as "the truth." We are simply revealing how our spouse's behavior was experienced as threatening.

In this position of openness, we are better prepared to bring the unconscious material of our narrative into conscious awareness. As we have learned, the story begins with unconscious material—memories and emotions—emerging from our right brain. As our narrative develops, it will seem more complete if we slow down long enough to engage with this unconscious material. How do we do this? Bonnie Badenoch, a marriage counselor, instructs us to invite this material into consciousness by paying attention to our bodily sensations, feelings, and behavioral impulses.[283] As we expand our story to include descriptions of physical experiences ("my stomach is in knots"), vulnerable feelings ("I am missing your attention"), and urges to act ("I am tempted to quit talking"), memories stored in our unconscious may come into awareness. As implicit memories become explicit, we become more skilled at separating the past from the present—in our lives and in our stories.

As our stories take on a greater ring of truth, they focus less on explanations and more on descriptions. We will spend less time explaining *why* our spouse acted (or failed to act) in a certain way. We will have less of a need to explain *why* we perceived the event a certain way. Instead of evaluating your spouse or yourself, your story will become more of a description. You will describe your own sensations, memories, feelings, and thoughts without evaluating them. You will describe your perception of your spouse without needing to evaluate your spouse or support your point of view.

As we incorporate the skills listed so far, we are more willing to move to a common story. It now becomes "our story." This approach requires a profound shift in our view of interactions. Instead of being seen as "the truth," our own personal story is simply "our perspective." As a result, we are able to hold our viewpoint with less tenacity. Our story is different because both points of view are welcomed and entertained. Both perspectives are treated as valid and worthy of consideration.

A common story sets the stage for moving from a negative to a positive story. Instead of seeing our spouse as bad or wrong, a positive story emphasizes the good times and accentuates our partner's positive traits.[284] It isn't that we don't experience bad times together or that our spouse doesn't have annoying characteristics, but a positive story avoids judgment. Instead of seeing our spouse as faulty, we offer an explanation that casts our spouse in a positive light.

Research is showing us that positive stories generate positive feelings in our marriage.[285] When we examine the neurobiology of narratives, we find that positive stories activate the left prefrontal cortex. Research by Richard Davidson reveals that greater activation in the left prefrontal cortex underlies positive emotions, while greater activity in the right prefrontal cortex is associated with negative emotions.[286] Thus, it comes as no surprise that positive stories result in greater positive emotions.

What is the connection between the elements of a truth-filled narrative—stepping back from our story, shifting to openness, recognizing unconscious material, focusing on descriptions, letting go of "my story," avoiding judgment—and a contemplative practice? We have learned that contemplation is about a special kind of attention. We learn to repeatedly distance ourselves from thoughts that float down the river of consciousness, as we observe them and return our attention to our intention. We avoid getting caught up in judgments of the thoughts that appear as we engage in Centering Prayer. We simply use our sacred word to let go of the thought and return to our intention. In prayer, as we watch the activities of the mind, we will notice the emergence of emotions and memories that have been hidden in our unconscious mind. The experience may burst upon the scene in the form of physical sensations. In Centering Prayer, we employ the same strategy with the Four Rs: resist no thought, retain no thought, react to no thought, return to the sacred word.

After many weeks of practicing Centering Prayer, Rachel was learning to distance herself from her stories about David. She was starting to question the truth of her stories, and focus more upon her role in their interactions. Perhaps David was withdrawing because she was putting too much pressure on him to talk. Could it be that David was less involved in parenting because she criticized the way he parented?

We noticed that the distance Rachel acquired through a contemplative practice was helping her build "our story." These narratives sounded very different from the ones she brought to therapy. The new stories sounded more like this: "David has a tendency to withdraw when I push him to talk about himself too soon after an upsetting event, and when he is not expressing himself, I get insecure, which shows up as pushiness. When I criticize David's parenting style, he is apt to be less involved in parenting. When he backs away from parenting, I feel alone, which reveals itself through criticism."

As we engage in a contemplative practice, we develop the trait of telling a story of truth. Daniel Siegel writes, "Here is the key: The truth sets us free."[287] Here he is quoting Jesus, who said, "The truth will set you free" (John 8:32). This is what we discover through Centering Prayer. We learn to reach a level that is deeper than our own mental activity and narratives. We enter a spiritual dimension where we commune with God in silence. At this level, as we step away from the activities of our mind and enter into truth. Then, as we return to our normal level of thinking, hopefully we tell stories that are filled with greater truth.

Try this:

1. Notice a criticism that you have of your spouse (either spoken or just thought). Look at this issue in terms of how your spouse was raised. How does introducing this perspective alter the story you tell about your spouse?

2. Identify a strong negative reaction that you had to your spouse's behavior this week. Think about how this intense response could be related to events from your own childhood. When you do this, you are beginning to see that your story about your spouse is as much about you as it is about them.

3. Sometime this week, notice a negative story that you have about your spouse. Notice if your story explains why your spouse was acting in a way that you found unpleasant. (Example: "My spouse did so-and-so because she is selfish.") Now, retell this story by describing how you responded to your spouse's behavior. (Example: "When my spouse did so-and-so, my stomach felt tight. I felt irritated. Her behavior reminded me of how my father treated me as a child. My first instinct was to say something critical.") See how the story changes.

4. Catch yourself creating a positive story about your spouse this week.

CHAPTER 20

Resonance

Attuned couples link together in mental lovemaking, a
joining of minds, in which two people create that beautiful
resonant sense of becoming a "we."
—*Daniel Siegel, Mindsight*

Anyone who loves his wife loves himself.
—*Ephesians 5:28*

While in high school, like so many of my peers, I fell in love . . . with the guitar. I soon found out that to play this glamorous instrument I had to learn a basic skill. That is, I needed to learn how to tune the guitar. My teacher taught me about standard tuning, a tuning method that gave each string a specific pitch. When the guitar was properly tuned, each string vibrated at a certain frequency. The next step in playing the guitar was learning how to play chords—that is, playing several notes together. If the guitar was tuned correctly, the pitches of the different notes being played together created a pleasant sound. In other words, the notes were vibrating in harmony. The notes had resonance. However, if I had not tuned the guitar properly, the chord had a discordant sound. The notes lacked harmony and resonance.

Learning to be happily married is much like learning to play the guitar. The entire process depends on proper tuning. This—the tuning of yourself—has been the primary focus of this book. We have focused most of our attention on the proper functioning of our mind. Through the regular process of contemplative prayer, our goal has been to alter the vibrations of our mind. We want to avoid a mind that vibrates too rapidly or too slowly. Instead, we want to set our mind at the proper frequency.

If contemplative prayer focuses on tuning the individual, marriage is playing the chords. Marriage is about the bringing together of two different notes—you and your spouse. If each note is tuned at the proper frequency, they can be played together and the chord makes a wonderful sound. The chord is in harmony.

Resonance is about the bringing together of two different parts.[288] When the two parts are properly tuned, the two become linked as one; they together create one harmonic sound. This concept of oneness within marriage shows up as one of the earliest teachings in Scripture: "For this reason a man will leave his father and mother and be united to his wife, and they will become one flesh" (Genesis 2:24). Jesus, familiar with this Jewish teaching about marriage, picked up on this concept of oneness (Matthew 19:5; Mark 10:8).

Being connected, or one, is a difficult concept for us to grasp. My mind—because of its limitations—shows me a world where my spouse and I are separate. I am over here, and my spouse is over there. I do my thing, and she does her thing. I take care of myself, while she takes care of herself. I am not responsible for her, and she is not responsible for me. We are each responsible for ourselves. With this kind of thinking, ultimately we find ourselves trapped in a box of "me, my, and mine."

During the early weeks in our work together, Steve and Linda relied primarily upon "me, my, and mine" words. He had his way of handling finances, and she had hers. He preferred one style of parenting, while she preferred another When it came to conflicts, he thought they should be handled one way, while she approached them from a different angle. Steve was convinced that his way was best, and Linda was sure that she was right. They were both stuck in a box.

When I look for the builder of this box, I find the *self*. You will remember from chapter 2 that the self has two predominant operations. First, it allows us to see the activities of the mind. The self provides us with an awareness of our bodily responses, emotional reactions, memories, and commentaries. Second, the self then goes on to conclude: "I am these sensations, thoughts, and feelings." This conclusion gives us the feeling that our body and mind exist independently from others with whom we are interacting; we are separate, unique. This—when we begin to believe that we are separate from our spouse—is when the self has boxed us in. The self has led us to believe something that is not true.

Contemplative prayer and modern science suggest that there is a way out of the box. Freedom comes from resonance, by seeing that we are part of a larger unit. Liberation comes as we move from *me* to *we*. We are no longer two separate notes sending out unrelated sound waves, we are a chord creating harmonious music. This sound of harmony comes with greater marital satisfaction. John Gottman writes, "The more people used the we-ness words, the happier their relationship was."[289]

The trait of resonance, which reveals itself in several ways, first shows up in our language. Whereas terms like *me, my,* and *mine* were products of an old mentality, one that emphasized our sense of separation, we now find words like *we, us,* and *our* showing up more often in our speech.[290] With an emphasis on connectivity, we increasingly notice ourselves using we-ness words, terms that builds a sense of togetherness and unity.

We-ness also shows up in how we tell our narratives. Before we began our practice of contemplative prayer, our mind was fixated on one note: the note of self. Our stories had one primary purpose: self-protection. The narrative served the function of making us look good, which often meant that we had to make our spouse look bad. Our narrative was interested in one perspective: our own.

As our mind is tuned through Centering Prayer, we attempt to build a common story—a story-of-us. This altered narrative has several distinct qualities. First, its primary concern is protecting the relationship. Relinquishing the need to cast ourselves in a positive light, we are more willing to reveal our weaknesses. Second, it welcomes two perspectives: mine and yours. The story-of-us includes two perspectives now, and both perspectives have equal value. "Our story" is one that rings true for both my spouse and me.

With time, Steve and Linda moved toward "our story." As they improved their ability to stay open to the other person's perspective, they began to find common ground. Over a period of weeks, instead of announcing, "This is how I handle money," they began to say, "This is our way of managing money." In place of the phrase, "I parent this way," I began to hear the expression, "This is how we co-parent." More and more, I heard them stating, "This is how *we* handle our conflicts."

Just the other day, my wife and I found ourselves working toward a story-of-us. At first, we were caught in old mental and narrative habits. We were each fixated on our own perspectives, seeing the other person as "wrong." However, in an effort to interrupt old patterns, we stopped and took ten minutes to create "our story." This account had three guidelines: It had to be a story of facts—no interpretations or beliefs. It had to be written down. And we had to agree on each part of the account. If we couldn't agree on a "fact," then it was excluded from the narrative. In a relatively short time, the process helped us move from discord to harmony.

The trait of resonance also shows up in how we take care of our spouse. The old thinking is, "I take care of myself, and you take care of yourself." However, resonance leads us to the idea that my own well-being rests in providing you with comfort, safety, and security. Marriage counselors Marion Solomon and Stan Tatkin put it this way: "The best way for people to meet their own needs is by taking care of each other."[291]

This approach rests upon the assumption that we are interconnected and we must look after one another. As the Apostle Paul said, "Husbands ought to love their wives in the same way as they do their own bodies. Anyone who loves his wife loves himself" (Ephesians 5:28). When we take care of our spouse, we are attending to ourselves.

Since we are one, we are not immune to the mental activities of our spouse. Both science and contemplative thought are telling us that our minds are connected. The energy and contents of our spouse's mind flows into our own, and we share our partner's emotional turmoil. The sensations of their bodies affect us personally. Therefore, it is essential that we become skilled at reading the other person's body language. Once we read distress in our spouse's facial expression, posture, or tone of voice, we must respond. We cannot allow the distress to go unattended. Ignoring the signals for a day is way too long.[292] Remember, by turning to and looking after our spouse, we are tending to ourselves.

Findings from neuroscience are showing us that there is a neurobiology of "we." As Daniel Siegel claims, "Resonance allows us to feel each other's feelings."[293] How do emotions flow between spouses? According to neuroscience, mirror neurons, located in the brain cortex, are involved in the process of picking up the emotions of our spouse.[294] Research suggests that mirror neurons act in the following way.[295] First, I observe my wife engaged in a typical behavior; for example, laughter. Then, neurons fire in my cortex—the same ones that would ignite if I were laughing. (Remember, for now, I am just watching and listening to my spouse.) Next, I feel the urge to imitate my wife; that is, to join in the laughter.

It seems that mirror neurons allow us to sense not only the action that is coming next, but also the emotion that underlies the behavior. The mirror neurons allow us to soak in the emotional state of our spouse. In this example, my wife was feeling excited and happy. Without intending it, because of mirror neurons, I began to feel the same happiness as my spouse.

How is this trait of resonance related to the practice of contemplative prayer? In contemplative prayer, there are moments when the mind ceases its chatter and becomes still, and our sense of separation from

God disappears. For an instant, we recognize that we are already in the divine embrace. For an instant, we experience divine union. Entering into the mystery of oneness with God opens us to the possibility of unity with our spouse. The daily practice of letting go that occurs in contemplative prayer translates into a trait of resonance which allows us to move from a sense of "me" to the experience of "we."

Neuroscientist Andrew Newberg tells us more about how contemplation alters the brain and provides us with resonance.[296] His studies show that the parietal lobe—the top section of the cortex that gives us a sense of self in relation to time, space, and objects in the world—is altered by contemplative practice. As activity in the parietal lobe slows down through contemplation, changes occur in brain functioning. Our perception of time and space may be altered, as we experience a feeling of timelessness and spacelessness. As our sense of self begins to dissolve so does our sense of separation from others, and we begin to feel unified with others and the world. This is the experience of resonance, the sense of being in harmony with something bigger than yourself.

Try this:

1. Notice when you and your spouse are working in harmony this week. Then, observe the times when you are not working together. Don't judge yourself. Just practice being aware of what is happening.

2. Be aware of the story you create when it seems that you and your spouse are not working well together. Do you create a narrative that blames your spouse for the disharmony?

3. Catch yourself using the words me, my, and mine this week. Then, notice when you use the words we, us, and our. Do the words you use affect how you feel?

4. One time when you are with your spouse this week, notice how they are feeling. Then, notice how you are feeling. Have your spouse's emotions flowed over to you? In other words, have you absorbed your spouse's emotions?

CHAPTER 21

Trustworthiness

*Trust is a state of receptivity akin to the notion
of love without fear.*
—Daniel Siegel, *The Mindful Therapist*

*A wife of noble character who can find?
She is worth far more than rubies.
Her husband has full confidence in her and
lacks nothing of value.
She brings him good, not harm, all the days of her life.*
—*Proverbs 31:11–12*

Science has discovered the most widely desired characteristic of a spouse, and that trait is trustworthiness.[297] Trustworthiness means that we have our spouse's best interests at heart rather than our own self-interests. Undoubtedly, this quality engenders and fits with a corresponding characteristic in our spouse: trust. Trust is the belief by our partner that we have their best interests at heart. Trust is the confidence that we are there for them.

Trustworthiness is the final and most significant trait that we will address in this book. It is the most important relational tool that we can bring to our marriage. It is the foundation upon which we build our marriage. Without it, our marriage will become boring, barren, and bleak. However, with it, we will keep finding ways to heal the hurts that happen between us. We will discover ways out of painful and difficult times. And we will be able to reconstruct our relationship when change is needed.

Fortunately, the trait of trustworthiness does not stand alone. It is built upon and has a reciprocal relationship with the other five traits we have examined: resonance, storytelling, presence, attunement, and calmness.

Resonance is an essential element of trustworthiness, and arises from the awareness that we are inextricably linked to our spouse. As a result, we are responsible for their care. This requires that we move from a position of "me" to one of "we." These changes in our mentality enable our spouse to entrust themselves into our care and protection knowing that we will be there for them. Our spouse's experience of this resonance assures them that we will not place our own interests first. They are free to feel safe and secure with us.

Telling stories that have the ring of truth assures our spouse that we are trustworthy. As we have seen, stories of truth are characterized by four elements. First, they attempt to capture "our story" rather than "my story." The emergence of resonance frees us from the normal mind's emphasis on "me, my, and mine." Instead, there is now a willingness to introduce our spouse's point of view alongside our own perspective. Second, stories of truth resist a negative turn. We have learned that the normal mind has a tendency to construct stories of blame. However, in an effort to speak the truth, we resist this tendency.

This leads us to the next characteristic of truth-telling in storytelling. Our narratives shift from a self-protective to vulnerable stance. This means that we are willing to be open, to explore how a painful interaction intersects with harmful events from our past. Finally, stories of truth communicate acceptance rather than judgment. Where our old stories contained negative evaluations of our spouse, attacks, and pressure to change, now our spouse finds compassion and acceptance. I like this definition of acceptance: "Pain minus accusation equals acceptance."[298] The story may contain pain but is devoid of accusations. This type of story provides safety for our spouse. In this context, they can trust us.

Our trait of presence engenders in our spouse a feeling of trust. In the past, captured by the normal mind, we reacted to painful interactions. We either turned away in fear or attacked in anger. With presence, we are now able to turn toward our spouse when they are upset with us. We are not compelled to change the interaction so that it is more to our liking. With a feeling of compassion, we can ask this question: "What does my spouse need at this time?" Presence, rather than reactivity, has a calming effect on our spouse. Our ability to be there for them in a difficult time helps create a sense of safety and trust.

Attunement, the trait of responding effectively to our spouse's emotions, is essential for establishing a foundation of trust. We have learned that the normal mind is self-centered and self-protective. However, with the trait of attunement, we are able to turn our attention outward, to our spouse. We entertain the question: "What nonverbal emotional signals are they sending?" Without any judgment, we ask ourselves the questions: "What is my spouse feeling? How do they view the situation? What are they needing from me at this time?" With openness, we are willing to listen to and understand their perspectives and needs, and our responsiveness to their feelings generates security and trust, qualities that are essential to a happy marriage.

Finally, our spouse wants to know if we will be there for them when their threat system is activated and their body is out of balance. Do we have the ability to soothe and calm them, versus react negatively to them, when their body is in a high state of arousal? This is the final trait of calmness. In the past, our normal mind would have resisted our spouse when their threat response system was activated. We would have felt compelled to protect ourselves. However, we are now willing to stay engaged when we see physical signs that their body is out of balance. Perhaps we will provide our spouse with physical comfort or use a calm tone of voice when they are distressed. We realize that we are not responsible for changing our spouse's physically distressed state.

However, as we listen and try to understand, we do provide them with a calming presence.

As we examine the traits that create the conditions for trustworthiness, it becomes clear that trust rests upon the assumption that spouses are not separate entities. We are linked, and we rely upon each other. When my body and mind get out of balance, I need my spouse to calm my threat response system. When I am overwhelmed with negative emotions, I need my spouse to respond effectively to them. When I am feeling insecure, I need my spouse to offer a sense of presence. When I feel caught in an unhelpful story, I need my spouse to introduce a story of truth. And finally, when I am feeling disconnected and alone, I need my spouse to remind me that we are linked together as one. When my spouse provides these responses, I experience her as trustworthy and I respond in kind with trust.

Of course, I am not suggesting that we are not responsible for balancing our own mind. On the contrary, part II of this book is devoted to teaching us how we can retrain our mind through a regular practice of Centering Prayer. Instead, I am saying that we are responsible for helping our spouse restore balance to their mind. As we do so, we demonstrate that we are trustworthy. And as our spouse experiences us being there for them, they have trust in us.

Trustworthiness and trust have an amazing reciprocal relationship. When our spouse's mind falls out of balance, we demonstrate trustworthiness by helping them restore mental stability. This then builds trust in our spouse. When our spouse trusts us, we experience the benefits of that. As we saw in John Gottman's study, a wife's trust in her husband lowers the blood pressure for both marriage partners.[299] In my case, my wife benefits if I am trustworthy, but I also benefit (my blood pressure goes down) when my wife trusts me. Clearly, by taking care of my spouse, I am taking care of myself.

Throughout part III, I addressed the connection between a regular practice of Centering Prayer and the five elements that support trustworthiness. The trait of calmness is linked to our ability to still our bodies. In contemplative prayer, we learn to start with our body. As Father Keating instructs us, we need to "sit comfortably." The next trait, attunement, grows out of the regular contemplative practice of letting go. As Father Keating says, "Centering prayer is an exercise in letting go. That is all it is. It lays aside every thought."[300] The quality of presence is not only tied to letting go, it is also cultivated by the contemplative practice of openness. Telling the truth emerges from the attention that we develop during contemplative prayer. And finally, resonance is cultivated as the veil of separation disappears and we experience union with God.

Ultimately, trustworthiness is linked to love. When we are trustworthy, our spouse feels loved. When our spouse feels loved, there is no fear. This is what trust is: love without fear.[301]

We know that love and trust are in danger when the mind is operating out of fear. The good news is that the neurobiology of contemplation helps us understand how to turn off fear. Research reveals that contemplative practice activates circuits in the left prefrontal cortex and creates stronger connections between the left prefrontal cortex and the amygdala.[302] These changes to the brain seem to be responsible for restoring balance to the body and mind after an upsetting event. Contemplative prayer allows the mind to shift from fear to love, thus opening the door to trust.

Daniel Siegel notes that trust opens the doorway to love in a relationship.[303] Isn't this where we ultimately want to reside, in a marriage that is full of love, safety, and security? The journey is not an easy one; we have learned of the obstacles that our mind, which can easily fall out of balance, can create on the way to this destination. Because of its tendency to be self-protective, it can interfere with our desire to establish a satisfying and fulfilling marriage. However, we have discovered that there is hope. By employing an approach of mind over marriage, we can achieve both internal and interpersonal well-being. Our mind can be renewed through a regular practice of Centering Prayer. The skills that we acquire through contemplation have the power to produce personal traits that we can apply to our marriage. Ultimately, changing our mind through contemplative prayer can change our marriage. Through a regular practice of Centering Prayer, I am convinced that you will find this to be true.

Acknowledgments

Even though my name is on the front of this book, I know that this project could not have come together without the help and support of many people. First, I am extremely grateful for Ana, my wife, and Elise and Juliana, my daughters, because they were the ones who inspired me to begin this work. They believed that I could write this book long before I believed it myself. They persuaded me that I had something valuable to share with readers. Whenever I became discouraged during the process of getting the book published, I obtained strength through their immovable confidence in this project and me. Over the many months it took me to compose the chapters of this book, they patiently welcomed my requests to read and provide feedback on the most recent section.

In the early days of this undertaking, my friend Mary Caldwell provided me with important advice and encouragement. Her suggestion to weave stories of couples into the book drastically altered its style and character. In addition, as she read early drafts of the book, Mary helped me believe in my writing abilities and the unique nature of this venture.

During the long process of writing and getting the book published, I am so thankful for the other people who consistently showed interest and championed this project. My best friend, David Litteral, my counseling colleague, Jared Massanari, and my sister, Marilyn Lane, were constant supporters. I also remember with gratitude my Mom, Betty Blanton, who provided steady backing and reassurance until her untimely death in the middle of this project. She extended resolute interest in the latest developments of the book and was convinced that I would get it published. I wish she were here today to see it coming to completion, but perhaps she saw it finished long before I did.

I am indebted to Father Thomas Keating, who agreed to read the manuscript as it was nearing completion. Father Thomas is one of my heroes because centering prayer, which he developed, provided much of the inspiration for this project. I was honored that he liked the manner in which I applied centering prayer to intimate relationships. When Father Thomas offered to recommend the manuscript to the folks at Lantern Books, I felt even more grateful.

Thanks go to my editor, Wendy Lee, and her team at Lantern Books. She skillfully led me through the activity of completing the manuscript and getting it ready for publication. I so appreciate her kind and thoughtful guidance through this process.

I also want to thank Montreat College for providing me with a sabbatical experience. Without time, a book cannot be written, so I am thankful for this gift given to me by the college.

As I complete these acknowledgments, I am filled with gratitude for all the individuals who supported me in various ways throughout this process. Without their help, I know that this book would never have been completed or published. This is my way of expressing thanks to all these people who I love and upon whom I depend.

Notes

1 A. Christensen and N. S. Jacobson, *Reconcilable Differences* (New York: Guilford Press, 2000).

2 G. G. May, *Will and Spirit* (New York: HarperCollins, 1982).

3 D. J. Siegel, *The Mindful Therapist* (New York: W. W. Norton, 2010).

4 P. Gilbert, *The Compassionate Mind* (Oakland, CA: New Harbinger, 2009).

5 Siegel, *The Mindful Therapist.*

6 J. O'Donohue, *Eternal Echoes* (New York: HarperCollins, 1999), 107.

7 Gilbert, *The Compassionate Mind*; D. J. Siegel, *Mindsight* (New York: Random House, 2010).

8 M. J. Meadow, *Christian Insight Meditation* (Boston: Wisdom Publications, 2007); J. O'Donohue, *Anam Cara* (New York: HarperCollins, 1997); G. G. May, *The Dark Night of the Soul* (New York: HarperCollins, 2004); D. G. Benner, *Opening to God* (Downers Grove, IL: InterVarsity Press, 2010); T. Keating, *Open Mind, Open Heart* (New York: Continuum, 1986).

9 R. Rohr, *The Naked Now* (New York: Crossroad Publishing Company, 2009).

10 Siegel, *The Mindful Therapist.*

11 Siegel, *Mindsight.*

12 O'Donohue, *Eternal Echoes.*

13 Benner, *Opening to God.*

14 Keating, *Open Mind, Open Heart*.

15 R. Rohr, *Everything Belongs* (New York: Crossroad Publishing Company, 1999).

16 J. M. Gottman, *The Science of Trust* (New York: W. W. Norton, 2011).

17 T. Merton, *New Seeds of Contemplation* (New York: New Directions, 1961), 112.

18 J. O'Donohue, *Beauty* (New York: HarperCollins, 2004).

19 T. Keating, *Manifesting God* (New York: Lantern Books, 2005).

20 Rohr, *Everything Belongs*, 66.

21 A. Wallace, *Minding Closely* (Ithaca, NY: Snow Lion Publications, 2011), xv.

22 Keating, *Open Mind, Open Heart*, 4.

23 Gottman, *The Science of Trust*.

24 M. Solomon and S. Tatkin, *Love and War in Intimate Relationships* (New York: W.W. Norton, 2011).

25 Siegel, *The Mindful Therapist*; Solomon and Tatkin, *Love and War in Intimate Relationships*.

26 Gottman, *The Science of Trust*.

27 D. Gehart and E. E. McCollum, "Inviting Therapeutic Presence," in *Mindfulness and the Therapeutic Relationship*, ed. S. F. Hick and T. Bien (New York: Guilford Press, 2008), 176–94.

28 Gottman, *The Science of Trust*.

29 Ibid.

30 Ibid.

31 Siegel, *The Mindful Therapist*.

32 Solomon and Tatkin, *Love and War in Intimate Relationships*.

33 Keating, *Open Mind, Open Heart*.

34 O'Donohue, *Eternal Echoes*.

35 M. Laird, *Into the Silent Land* (New York: Oxford University Press. 2006).

36 Keating, *Open Mind, Open Heart*.

37 D. J. Wallin, *Attachment in Psychotherapy* (New York: Guilford Press, 2007).

38 Solomon and Tatkin, *Love and War in Intimate Relationships*.

39 Ibid., 73–78.

40 A. Damasio, *Self Comes to Mind* (New York: Pantheon Books, 2010).

41 Siegel, *The Mindful Therapist*.

42 Damasio, *Self Comes to Mind*.

43 May, *Will and Spirit*, 177.

44 Damasio, *Self Comes to Mind*.

45 Wallin, *Attachment in Psychotherapy*.

46 S. M. Johnson, *The Practice of Emotionally Focused Couple Therapy: Creating Connection* (New York: Brunner-Routledge, 2004).

47 Siegel, *The Mindful Therapist*.

48 Damasio, *Self Comes to Mind*.

49 D. G. Benner, *Soulful Spirituality* (Grand Rapids, MI: Brazos Press, 2011).

50 Keating, *Manifesting God*.

51 Damasio, *Self Comes to Mind*, 13.

52 Damasio, *Self Comes to Mind*.

53 O'Donohue, *Anam Cara*, 48.

54 Solomon and Tatkin, *Love and War in Intimate Relationships*.

55 Ibid.

56 Siegel, *Mindsight*.

57 Gottman, *The Science of Trust*.

58 Siegel, *Mindsight*.

59 C. Trevarthen, "The Functions of Emotions in Infancy," in *The Healing Power of Emotions*, ed. D. Fosha, D. Siegel, and M. Solomon (New York: W. W. Norton, 2009), 55–85.

60 D. Fosha, "Emotion and Recognition at Work," in *The Healing Power of Emotions*, ed. D. Fosha, D. Siegel, and M. Solomon (New York: W. W. Norton, 2009), 172–203.

61 Laird, *Into the Silent Land*, 45.

62 O'Donohue, *Anam Cara*, 48.

63 Solomon and Tatkin, *Love and War in Intimate Relationships*.

64 B. Badenoch, *The Brain-Savvy Therapist's Workbook* (New York: W. W. Norton, 2011).

65 Damasio, *Self Comes to Mind.*

66 May, *The Dark Night of the Soul.*

67 Solomon and Tatkin, *Love and War in Intimate Relationships.*

68 Rohr, *The Naked Now.*

69 T. Keating, *Invitation to Love* (New York: Continuum, 2000).

70 Siegel, *Mindsight.*

71 D. Ackerman, *An Alchemy of Mind* (New York: Scribner, 2004).

72 O'Donohue, *Eternal Echoes,* 178.

73 Gottman, *The Science of Trust,* 192.

74 B. Badenoch, *Being a Brain-Wise Therapist* (New York: W. W. Norton, 2008).

75 Ibid.

76 Solomon and Tatkin, *Love and War in Intimate Relationships.*

77 Ibid.

78 Badenoch, *The Brain-Savvy Therapist's Workbook.*

79 Keating, *Invitation to Love.*

80 Gilbert, *The Compassionate Mind.*

81 Badenoch, *Being a Brain-Wise Therapist.*

82 Damasio, *Self Comes to Mind.*

83 Ibid.

84 Siegel, *The Mindful Therapist.*

85 O'Donohue, *Anam Cara.*

86 L. Cozolino, *The Neuroscience of Psychotherapy* (New York: W. W. Norton, 2010).

87 Wallin, *Attachment in Psychotherapy.*

88 Solomon and Tatkin, *Love and War in Intimate Relationships.*

89 Rohr, *Everything Belongs,* 61.

90 L. Cozolino, *The Neuroscience of Human Relationships* (New York: W. W. Norton, 2006).

91 Gilbert, *The Compassionate Mind.*

92 Keating, *Invitation to Love.*

93 Ackerman, *An Alchemy of Mind*.

94 Badenoch, *The Brain-Savvy Therapist's Workbook*.

95 A. Damasio, *The Feeling of What Happens* (New York: Houghton Mifflin Harcourt, 1999), 185.

96 Keating, *Invitation to Love*.

97 A. Newberg and M. R. Waldman, *How God Changes Your Brain* (New York: Ballantine Books, 2009), 137.

98 M. R. Leary, *The Curse of Self* (New York: Oxford University Press, 2004).

99 Damasio, *The Feeling of What Happens*.

100 O'Donohue, *Beauty*, 137.

101 Badenoch, *The Brain-Savvy Therapist's Workbook*.

102 Ackerman, *An Alchemy of Mind*.

103 D. Bennett, *Consciousness Explained* (Boston: Little, Brown, 1999), 417.

104 Solomon and Tatkin, *Love and War in Intimate Relationships*, 256.

105 Wallin, *Attachment in Psychotherapy*.

106 Gottman, *The Science of Trust*, 212.

107 T. Keating, *Manifesting God* (New York: Lantern Books, 2005).

108 D. J. Siegel, *The Mindful Brain* (New York: W. W. Norton, 2007).

109 J. Freedman and G. Combs, "Narrative Couple Therapy," in *Clinical Handbook of Couple Therapy*, ed. A. S. Gurman (New York: Guilford Press, 2008), 229–57.

110 Christensen and Jacobson, *Reconcilable Differences*.

111 Keating, *Open Mind, Open Heart*.

112 R. A. Watson, "Toward Union in Love: The Contemplative Spiritual Tradition and Contemporary Psychoanalytic Theory in the Formation of Persons," in *Spiritual Formation, Counseling, and Psychotherapy*, ed. T. W. Hall and M. R. McMinn (New York: Nova Science Publishers, 2003), 53–68.

113 T. Merton, *The Wisdom of the Desert* (New York: New Directions, 1960).

114 Solomon and Tatkin, *Love and War in Intimate Relationships*.

115 Siegel, *Mindsight*.

116 Johnson, *The Practice of Emotionally Focused Couple Therapy*.

117 Christensen and Jacobson, *Reconcilable Differences*.

118 Ibid., 80.

119 Solomon and Tatkin, *Love and War in Intimate Relationships*.

120 Ibid.

121 Johnson, *The Practice of Emotionally Focused Couple Therapy*.

122 Siegel, *The Mindful Therapist*.

123 W. B. Yeats, "The Wild Swans at Coole" (New York: Macmillan, 1919).

124 O'Donohue, *Anam Cara*.

125 O'Donohue, *Beauty*, 132.

126 Keating, *Manifesting God*.

127 H. Nouwen, *Here and Now* (New York: Crossroad Publishing Company, 1994).

128 G. G. May, *Care of Mind, Care of Spirit* (New York: HarperCollins, 1992).

129 C. Bourgeault, *Centering Prayer and Inner Awakening* (Cambridge, MA: Cowley Publications, 2004).

130 *The Cloud of Unknowing*, trans. C. A. Butcher (Boston: Shambhala Publications, 2009).

131 May, *The Dark Night of the Soul*.

132 Meadow, *Christian Insight Meditation*.

133 May, *The Dark Night of the Soul*.

134 May, *Will and Spirit*, 35.

135 Benner, *Soulful Spirituality*, 109.

136 O'Donohue, *Eternal Echoes*, 196.

137 Merton, *New Seeds of Contemplation*.

138 Bourgeault, *Centering Prayer and Inner Awakening*.

139 Merton, *New Seeds of Contemplation*.

140 Keating, *Open Mind, Open Heart*.

141 Bourgeault, *Centering Prayer and Inner Awakening*.

142 Ibid., 13.

143 J. Finley, *Christian Meditation* (New York: HarperCollins, 2004).

144 Keating, *Open Mind, Open Heart,* 139.

145 Keating, *Open Mind, Open Heart.*

146 Keating, *Open Mind, Open Heart,* 139.

147 J. Joyce, *Dubliners* (New York: Bantam Books, 1990), 84.

148 Benner, *Soulful Spirituality,* 82.

149 Damasio, *Self Comes to Mind.*

150 Finley, *Christian Meditation.*

151 C. S. Lewis, *The Screwtape Letters* (New York: Macmillan, 1961), 25.

152 M. B. Pennington, *Centered Living* (Liguori, MO: Liguori Publications, 1999).

153 Laird, *Into the Silent Land.*

154 O'Donohue, *Anam Cara.*

155 Laird, *Into the Silent Land,* 6.

156 Laird, *Into the Silent Land.*

157 Ibid., 38.

158 Laird, *Into the Silent Land.*

159 Ibid.

160 Laird, *Into the Silent Land,* 39.

161 Ibid.

162 Keating, *Manifesting God.*

163 M. B. Pennington, *Centering Prayer* (Liguori, MO: Liguori Publications, 1999).

164 R. S. Thomas, "The Moor," in *Collected Poems 1945–1990* (London: Dent, 1993), 166.

165 Bourgeault, *Centering Prayer and Inner Awakening,* 19.

166 O'Donohue, *Eternal Echoes.*

167 Keating, *Invitation to Love,* 90.

168 Keating, *Open Mind, Open Heart.*

169 Benner, *Opening to God.*

170 Laird, *Into the Silent Land,* 49.

171 Newberg and Waldman, *How God Changes Your Brain.*

172 Keating, *Open Mind, Open Heart.*

173 Ibid.

174 Ibid.

175 Ibid., 139.

176 *The Cloud of Unknowing,* 24.

177 Bourgeault, *Centering Prayer and Inner Awakening.*

178 Laird, *Into the Silent Land.*

179 Bourgeault, *Centering Prayer and Inner Awakening.*

180 Ibid., 24.

181 Keating, *Open Mind, Open Heart,* 39.

182 Laird, *Into the Silent Land.*

183 Keating, *Open Mind, Open Heart,* 39.

184 D. N. Stern, *The Present Moment in Psychotherapy and Everyday Life* (New York: W. W. Norton, 2006).

185 Bourgeault, *Centering Prayer and Inner Awakening,* 39–40.

186 Benner, *Opening to God.*

187 Finley, *Christian Meditation.*

188 Keating, *Open Mind, Open Heart,* 93.

189 Keating, *Invitation to Love.*

190 Bourgeault, *Centering Prayer and Inner Awakening.*

191 Laird, *Into the Silent Land,* 63.

192 Keating, *Open Mind, Open Heart,* 74.

193 Meadow, *Christian Insight Meditation.*

194 Bourgeault, *Centering Prayer and Inner Awakening.*

195 Keating, *Invitation to Love.*

196 Merton, *New Seeds of Contemplation.*

197 Keating, *Open Mind, Open Heart.*

198 Bourgeault, *Centering Prayer and Inner Awakening,* 39–40.

199 May, *Will and Spirit.*

200 Benner, *Opening to God,* 165.

201 Laird, *Into the Silent Land.*

202 Bourgeault, *Centering Prayer and Inner Awakening.*

203 Laird, *Into the Silent Land.*

204 O'Donohue, *Beauty*, 227.

205 O'Donohue, *Beauty.*

206 Ibid., 227.

207 May, *Will and Spirit*, 123.

208 Keating, *Open Mind, Open Heart*, 13.

209 Merton, *New Seeds of Contemplation*, 7.

210 Keating, *Open Mind, Open Heart*, 74.

211 Merton, *New Seeds of Contemplation*, 36.

212 T. Merton, *Contemplative Prayer* (New York: Doubleday, 1996), 67.

213 Keating, *Open Mind, Open Heart*, 59.

214 May, *Will and Spirit.*

215 Keating, *Open Mind, Open Heart.*

216 Finley, *Christian Meditation*, 99.

217 May, *Will and Spirit*, 6.

218 Merton, *New Seeds of Contemplation*, 119.

219 J. Thurber and E. B. White, *Is Sex Necessary?* (New York: Perennial Library, 1975), 185.

220 O'Donohue, *Anam Cara*, 8.

221 Rohr, *Everything Belongs*, 85.

222 O'Donohue, *Anam Cara*, 13.

223 Ibid., 7.

224 A. Einsten, A letter quoted in the *New York Times* (March 29, 1972).

225 Wallin, *Attachment in Psychotherapy*, 6.

226 P. Granqvist and L. A. Kirkpatrick, "Attachment and Religious Representations of Behavior," in *Handbook of Attachment, Second Edition: Theory, Research, and Clinical Applications*, ed. J. Cassidy and P. R. Shaver (New York: Guilford Press, 2008), 906–33.

227 Ibid.

228 Keating, *Manifesting God.*

229   B. Boyce. *The Mindfulness Revolution* (Boston: Shambhala Publications, 2011).

230   Ibid.

231   J. Kabat-Zinn, *Full Catastrophe Living* (New York: Dell Publishing, 1990).

232   Boyce, *The Mindfulness Revolution*.

233   R. J. Davidson and A. Harrington, *Visions of Compassion* (New York: Oxford University Press, 2002).

234   Benner, *Soulful Spirituality*.

235   Gehart and McCollum, "Inviting Therapeutic Presence"; J. L. Kristeller, "Spiritual Engagement as a Mechanism of Change in Mindfulness- and Acceptance-Based Interventions," in *Assessing Mindfulness and Acceptance Processes and Clients,* ed. R. A. Baer (Oakland, CA: Context Press, 2010), 155–84; C. J. Robins, H. Schmidt, and M. M. Linehan, "Dialectical Behavior Therapy," in *Mindfulness and Acceptance: Expanding the Cognitive-Behavioral Tradition,* ed. S. C. Hayes, V. M. Follette, and M. M. Linehan (New York: Guilford Press, 2004), 30–44; Siegel, *The Mindful Brain.*

236   A. Newberg, M. Pourdehnand, A. Alavi, and E. G. d'Aquili, "Cerebral Blood Flow During Meditative Prayer: Preliminary Findings and Methodological Issues," *Perceptual Motor Skills* (October 2, 2003): 625–30.

237   Newberg and Waldman, *How God Changes Your Brain.*

238   Siegel, *The Mindful Therapist.*

239   Ibid.

240   Gilbert, *The Compassionate Mind.*

241   Gottman, *The Science of Trust.*

242   R. W. Levenson and J. M. Gottman, "Physiology and Affective Predictors of Change in Relationship Satisfaction," *Journal of Personality and Social Psychology* 49, (1985): 85–94.

243   Solomon and Tatkin, *Love and War in Intimate Relationships.*

244   Ibid.

245 Ibid.; Gottman, *The Science of Trust.*

246 J. A. Coan, H. S. Schaefer, and R. J. Davidson, "Lending a Hand: Social Regulation of the Neural Response of Threat," *Psychological Science* 17, (2006): 1032–39.

247 K. M. Grewen, S. S. Girdler, J. Amico, and K. C. Light. "Effects of Partner Support on Resting Oxytocin, Cortisol, Norepinephrine, and Blood Pressure Before and After Warm Partner Contact," *Psychosomatic Medicine* 67, (2005): 531–38.

248 I. Habuschagne, K. L. Phan, A. Wood, M. Angstadt, P. Chua, M. Heinrichs, J. C. Stout, and P. J. Nathan, "Oxytocin Attenuates Amygdala Reactivity to Fear in Generalized Social Anxiety Disorder," *Neuropsychopharmacology* 35, (2010): 2403–13.

249 Solomon and Tatkin, *Love and War in Intimate Relationships.*

250 R. J. Davidson, J. Kabat-Zinn, J. Schumacher, M. A. Rosenkranz, D. Muller, S. F. Santorelli, F. Urbanowski, A. Harrington, K. Bonus, and J. F. Sheridan, "Alterations in Brain and Immune Function Produced by Mindfulness Meditation," *Psychosomatic Medicine* 65, (2003): 564–70.

251 J. W. Carson, K. M. Gill, and D. H. Baucom, "Self-Expansion as a Mediator of Relationship Improvements in a Mindfulness Intervention," *Journal of Marital and Family Therapy* 33, (2007): 517–28.

252 R. J. Davidson and S. Begley, *The Emotional Life of Your Brain* (New York: Hudson Street Press, 2012).

253 Solomon and Tatkin, *Love and War in Intimate Relationships.*

254 Ibid.

255 Gottman, *The Science of Trust.*

256 Ibid.

257 Ibid.

258 Davidson and Begley, *The Emotional Life of Your Brain.*

259 Ibid.

260 Siegel, *Mindsight.*

261 S. Shapiro, G. E. Schwartz, and G. Bonner, "Effects of Mindful-

ness-Based Stress Reduction on Medical and Premedical Students," *Journal of Behavioral Medicine* 21, (1998): 581–99.

262 S. Shapiro and K. Brown, *Mindfulness and Empathy* (Unpublished manuscript, 2007).

263 S. L. Shapiro and C. D. Izett, "Meditation: A Universal Tool for Cultivating Empathy," in *Mindfulness and the Therapeutic Relationship*, ed. S. F. Hick and T. Bien (New York: Guilford Press, 2008), 161–75.

264 This exercise was adapted from an exercise appearing in Davidson and Begley's *The Emotional Life of Your Brain*, 236–47.

265 Siegel, *Mindsight*.

266 Siegel, *The Mindful Therapist*, 26.

267 Siegel, *Mindsight*.

268 J. Kabat-Zinn, *Mindfulness for Beginners* (Boulder, CO: Sounds True, 2012), 123.

269 Siegel, *Mindsight*.

270 Kabat-Zinn, *Mindfulness for Beginners*.

271 Siegel, *Mindsight*.

272 O'Donohue, *Anam Cara*, 91.

273 Gehart and McCollum, "Inviting Therapeutic Presence."

274 Benner, *Soulful Spirituality*.

275 Ibid., 152.

276 Ibid., 146.

277 O'Donohue, *Anam Cara*, 7.

278 Siegel, *Mindsight*.

279 Davidson and Begley, *The Emotional Life of Your Brain*.

280 Gottman, *The Science of Trust*, 212.

281 Christensen and Jacobson, *Reconcilable Differences*.

282 Ibid.

283 Badenoch, *The Brain-Savvy Therapist's Workbook*.

284 Gottman, *The Science of Trust*.

285 Ibid.

286 Davidson and Begley, *The Emotional Life of Your Brain*.

287 Siegel, *The Mindful Therapist*, 90.

288 Siegel, *The Mindful Therapist*.

289 Gottman, *The Science of Trust*, 155.

290 Gottman, *The Science of Trust*.

291 Solomon and Tatkin, *Love and War in Intimate Relationships*, 176.

292 Ibid.

293 Siegel, *The Mindful Therapist*, 39.

294 Cozolino, *The Neuroscience of Human Relationships*.

295 Siegel, *The Mindful Therapist*.

296 Newberg and Waldman, *How God Changes Your Brain*.

297 Gottman, *The Science of Trust*.

298 Christensen and Jacobson, *Reconcilable Differences*, 104.

299 Gottman, *The Science of Trust*.

300 Keating, *Open Mind, Open Heart*, 74.

301 Siegel, *The Mindful Therapist*, 74.

302 Davidson and Begley, *The Emotional Life of Your Brain*.

303 Siegel, *The Mindful Therapist*, 78.

References

Ackerman, D. *An Alchemy of Mind: The Marvel and Mystery of the Brain*. New York: Scribner, 2004.

Badenoch, B. *The Brain-Savvy Therapist's Workbook*. New York: W. W. Norton, 2011.

———. *Being a Brain-Wise Therapist: A Practical Guide to Interpersonal Neurobiology*. New York: W. W. Norton, 2008.

Benner, D. G. *Soulful Spirituality: Becoming Fully Alive and Deeply Human*. Grand Rapids, MI: Brazos Press, 2011.

———. *Opening to God: Lectio Divina and Life as Prayer*. Downers Grove, IL: InterVarsity Press, 2010.

Bourgeault, C. *Centering Prayer and Inner Awakening*. Cambridge, MA: Cowley Publications, 2004.

Boyce, B., ed. *The Mindfulness Revolution: Leading Psychologists, Scientists, Artists, and Meditation Teachers on the Power of Mindfulness in Daily Life*. Boston: Shambhala Publications, 2011.

Carson, J. W., K. M. Carson, K. M. Gill, and D. H. Baucom. "Self-expansion as a Mediator of Relationship Improvements in a Mindfulness Intervention." *Journal of Marital and Family Therapy* 33, (2007): 517–28.

Christensen, A., and N. S. Jacobson. *Reconcilable Differences*. New York: Guilford Press, 2000.

The Cloud of Unknowing. Translated by C. A. Butcher. Boston: Shambhala Publications, 2009.

Coan, J. A., H. S. Schaefer, and R. J. Davidson. "Lending a Hand: Social

Regulation of the Neural Response of Threat." *Psychological Science* 17, (2006): 1032–39.

Cozolino, L. *The Neuroscience of Human Relationships: Attachment and the Developing Social Brain.* New York: W. W. Norton, 2006.

———. *The Neuroscience of Psychotherapy: Building and Rebuilding the Human Brain.* New York: W. W. Norton, 2010.

Damasio, A. *The Feeling of What Happens: Body and Emotion in the Making of Consciousness.* New York: Houghton Mifflin Harcourt, 1999.

———. *Self Comes to Mind: Constructing the Conscious Brain.* New York: Pantheon Books, 2010.

Davidson, R. J., and S. Begley. *The Emotional Life of Your Brain: How Its Unique Patterns Affect the Way You Think, Feel, and Live—and How You Can Change Them.* New York: Hudson Street Press, 2012.

Davidson, R. J., and A. Harrington. *Visions of Compassion: Western Scientists and Tibetan Buddhists Examine Human Nature.* New York: Oxford University Press, 2002.

Davidson, R. J., J. Kabat-Zinn, J. Schumacher, M. Rosenkranz, D. Muller, S. F. Santorelli, F. Urbanowski, A. Harrington, K. Bonus, and J. F. Sheridan. "Alterations in Brain and Immune Function Produced by Mindfulness Meditation." *Psychosomatic Medicine* 65, (2003): 564–70.

Dennett, D. C. *Consciousness Explained.* Boston: Little, Brown, 1991.

Finley, J. *Christian Meditation: Experiencing the Presence of God.* New York: HarperCollins, 2004.

Fosha, D. "Emotion and Recognition at Work." In *The Healing Power of Emotion: Affective Neuroscience, Development & Clinical Practice,* edited by D. Fosha, D. Siegel, and M. Solomon, 172–203. New York: W. W. Norton, 2009.

Freedman, J., and G. Combs. "Narrative Couple Therapy." In *Clinical Handbook of Couple Therapy,* edited by A. S. Gurman, 229–57. New York: Guilford Press, 2008.

Gehart, D., and E. E. McCollum. "Inviting Therapeutic Presence." In

Mindfulness and the Therapeutic Relationship, edited by S. F. Hick and T. Bien, 176–94. New York: Guilford Press, 2008.

Gilbert, P. *The Compassionate Mind: A New Approach to Life's Challenges*. Oakland, CA: New Harbinger Publications, 2009.

Gottman, J. M. *The Science of Trust: Emotional Attunement for Couples*. New York: W. W. Norton, 2011.

Granqvist, P., and L. A. Kirkpatrick. "Attachment and Religious Representations of Behavior." In *Handbook of Attachment, Second Edition: Theory, Research, and Clinical Applications*, edited by J. Cassidy and P. R. Shaver, 906–33. New York: Guilford Press, 2008.

Grewen, K. M., S. S. Girdler, J. Amico, and K. C. Light. "Effects of Partner Support on Resting Oxytocin, Cortisol, Norepinephrine, and Blood Pressure Before and After Warm Partner Contact." *Psychosomatic Medicine* 67, (2005): 531–38.

Habuschagne, I., K. L. Phan, A. Wood, M. Angstadt, P. Chua, M. Heinrichs, J. C. Stout, and P. J. Nathan. "Oxytocin Attenuates Amygdala Reactivity to Fear in Generalized Social Anxiety Disorder." *Neuropsychopharmacology* 35, (2010): 2403–13.

Johnson, S. M. *The Practice of Emotionally Focused Couple Therapy: Creating Connection*. New York: Brunner Routledge, 2004.

Joyce, J. *Dubliners*. New York: Bantam Books, 1990.

Kabat-Zinn, J. *Full Catastrophe Living: Using the Wisdom of Your Body and Mind to Face Stress, Pain, and Illness*. New York: Dell Publishing, 1990.

———. *Mindfulness for Beginners: Reclaiming the Present Moment—and Your Life*. Boulder, CO: Sounds True, 2012.

Keating, T. *Invitation to Love: The Way of Christian Contemplation*. New York: Continuum Publishing Company, 2000.

———. *Manifesting God*. New York: Lantern Books, 2005.

———. *Open Mind, Open Heart*. New York: Continuum Publishing Company, 1986.

Kristeller, J. L. "Spiritual Engagement as a Mechanism of Change in Mindfulness- and Acceptance-Based Interventions." In *Assessing*

Mindfulness and Acceptance Processes in Clients: Illuminating the Theory and Practice of Change, edited by R. A. Baer, 155–84. Oakland, CA: Context Press, 2010.

Laird, M. *Into the Silent Land: A Guide to the Christian Practice of Contemplation.* New York: Oxford University Press. 2006.

Leary, M. R. *The Curse of Self: Self-Awareness, Egotism, and the Quality of Human Life.* New York: Oxford University Press, 2004.

Levenson, R. W., and J. M. Gottman. "Physiology and Affective Predictors of Change in Relationship Satisfaction." *Journal of Personality and Social Psychology* 49, (1985): 85–94.

Lewis, C. S. *The Screwtape Letters.* New York: Macmillan, 1961.

May, G. G. *Care of Mind, Care of Spirit: A Psychiatrist Explores Spiritual Direction.* New York: HarperCollins, 1992.

———. *The Dark Night of the Soul: A Psychiatrist Explores the Connection Between Darkness and Spiritual Growth.* New York: HarperCollins, 2004.

———. *Will and Spirit: A Contemplative Psychology.* New York: HarperCollins, 1982.

Meadow, M. J. *Christian Insight Meditation: Following in the Footsteps of John of the Cross.* Boston: Wisdom Publications. 2007.

Merton, T. *Contemplative Prayer.* New York: Doubleday, 1996.

———. *New Seeds of Contemplation.* New York: New Directions, 1961.

———. *The Wisdom of the Desert.* New York: New Directions, 1960.

Newberg, A., and M. R. Waldman. *How God Changes Your Brain: Breakthrough Findings from a Leading Neuroscientist.* New York: Ballantine Books, 2009.

Newberg, A., M. Pourdehnand, A. Alavi, and E. G. d'Aquili. "Cerebral Blood Flow During Meditative Prayer: Preliminary Findings and Methodological Issues." *Perceptual Motor Skills* (October 2, 2003): 625–30.

Nouwen, H. *Here and Now: Living in the Spirit.* New York: Crossroad Publishing Company, 1994.

O'Donohue, J. *Anam Cara: A Book of Celtic Wisdom.* New York: HarperCollins, 1997.

———. *Beauty: The Invisible Embrace.* New York: HarperCollins, 2004.

———. *Eternal Echoes: Celtic Reflections on Our Yearning to Belong.* New York: HarperCollins, 1999.

Pennington, M. B. *Centered Living: The Way of Centering Prayer.* Liguori, MO: Liguori Publications, 1999.

Robins, C. J., H. Schmidt, and M. M. Linehan. "Dialectical Behavior Therapy." In *Mindfulness and Acceptance: Expanding the Cognitive-Behavioral Tradition,* edited by S. C. Hayes, V. M. Follette, and M. M. Linehan, 1–44. New York: Guilford Press, 2004.

Rohr, R. *Everything Belongs: The Gift of Contemplative Prayer.* New York: Crossroad Publishing Company, 1999.

———. *The Naked Now: Learning to See as the Mystics See.* New York: Crossroad Publishing Company, 2009.

Shapiro, S., and K. Brown. *Mindfulness and Empathy.* Unpublished manuscript, 2007.

Shapiro, S. L., and C. D. Izett. "Meditation: A Universal Tool for Cultivating Empathy." In *Mindfulness and the Therapeutic Relationship,* edited by S. F. Hick and T. Bien, 161–75. New York: Guilford Press, 2008.

Shapiro, S., G. E. Schwartz, and G. Bonner. "Effects of Mindfulness-Based Stress Reduction on Medical and Premedical Students." *Journal of Behavioral Medicine* 21, (1998): 581–99.

Siegel, D. J. *Mindsight: The New Science of Personal Transformation.* New York: Random House, 2010.

———. *The Mindful Brain: Reflection and Attunement in the Cultivation of Well-Being.* New York: W. W. Norton, 2007.

———. *The Mindful Therapist: A Clinician's Guide to Mindsight and Neural Integration.* New York: W. W. Norton, 2010.

Solomon, M., and S. Tatkin. *Love and War in Intimate Relationships: Connection, Disconnection, and Mutual Regulation in Couple Therapy.* New York: W. W. Norton, 2011.

Stern, D. N. *The Present Moment in Psychotherapy and Everyday Life.* New York: W. W. Norton, 2006.

Trevarthen, C. "The Functions of Emotions in Infancy." In *The Healing Power of Emotion: Affective Neuroscience, Development & Clinical Practice*, edited by D. Fosha, D. Siegel, and M. Solomon, 55–85. New York: W. W. Norton, 2009.

Wallace, B. A. *Minding Closely: The Four Applications of Mindfulness.* Ithaca, NY: Snow Lion Publications, 2011.

Wallin, D. J. *Attachment in Psychotherapy.* New York: Guilford Press, 2007.

Watson, R. A. "Toward Union in Love: The Contemplative Spiritual Tradition and Contemporary Psychoanalytic Theory in the Formation of Persons." In *Spiritual Formation, Counseling, and Psychotherapy,* edited by T. W. Hall and M. R. McMinn, 53–68. New York: Nova Science Publishers, 2003.

About the Author

P. GREGG BLANTON, EDD, is a professor of Psychology & Human Services at
Montreat College and an adjunct professor at
Gordon-Conwell Theological Seminary. As
a licensed marriage and family therapist, he
maintains a private practice, provides super-
vision, offers training programs, and conducts
retreats for couples. He lives in Asheville, NC,
with his wife and two children.

http://greggblanton.intuitwebsites.com/

About the Publisher

LANTERN BOOKS was founded in 1999 on the principle of living with a greater depth and commitment to the preservation of the natural world. In addition to publishing books on animal advocacy, vegetarianism, religion, and environmentalism, Lantern is dedicated to printing books in the U.S. on recycled paper and saving resources in day-to-day operations. Lantern is honored to be a recipient of the highest standard in environmentally responsible publishing from the Green Press Initiative.

www.lanternbooks.com

CPSIA information can be obtained
at www.ICGtesting.com
Printed in the USA
FFOW04n1941131114
8752FF